WICCA & TAROT FOR BEGINNERS

2 Books in 1: Learn Wiccan Magic, Rituals, Spells, Beliefs, Symbolism, Crystal Magic and Tarot Divination

Lisa Miller

© Copyright 2020 by Lisa Miller. All rights reserved.

The material contained herein is presented with the intent of furnishing pertinent and relevant information and knowledge on the topic with the sole purpose of providing entertainment. The author should thus not be considered an expert on the topic in this material despite any claims to such expertise, first-hand knowledge and any other reasonable claim to specific knowledge on the material contained herein. The information presented in this work has been researched to ensure its reasonable accuracy and validity. Nevertheless, it is advisable to consult with a duly licensed professional in the area pertaining to this topic, or any other covered in this book, in order to ensure the quality and validity of the advice and/or techniques contained in this material.

This is a legally binding statement as deemed so by the Committee of Publishers Association and the American Bar Association in the United States. Any reproduction, transmission, copying or otherwise duplication of the material contained in this work are in violation of current copyright legislation. No physical or digital copies of this work, both total and partial, may not be done without the Publisher's express written consent. All additional rights are reserved by the publisher of this work.

The data, facts and description of events forthwith shall be considered as accurate unless the work is deemed to be a work of fiction. In any event, the Publisher is exempt of responsibility for any use of the information contained in the present work on the part of the user. The author and Publisher may not be deemed liable, under any circumstances, for the events resulting from the observance of the advice, tips, techniques and any other contents presented herein.

Given the informational and entertainment nature of the content presented in this work, there is no guarantee as to the quality and validity of the information. As such, the contents of this work are deemed as universal. No use of copyrighted material is used in this work. Any references to other trademarks are done so under fair use and by no means represent an endorsement of such trademarks or their holder.

TABLE OF CONTENTS

WICCA CRYSTAL MAGIC
Learn Wiccan Beliefs, Rituals & Magic, and How to Use Wiccan Spells Using Crystals & Mineral Stones

Introduction 2
Chapter 1 *Introducing Wicca* 3

    What Is Wicca? 3
    Thirteen Principles of Witchcraft 5
    History of Wicca 10
    What Wicca and Wiccans Are Not 12
    What Wiccans and Wicca Are 15
    Branches of Wicca 17
    Core Beliefs 21

Chapter 2 *Terms To Know* 23

    Absent Healing 23
    Acolyte 23
    Adept 23
    Akasha 23
    Akashic Records 24
    Altar 24
    Anima 24
    Amulet 24
    Animism 24
    Ankh 25
    An-shet 25
    Apprentice 25
    Aspects 25
    Asperger 25
    Astral Body 26
    Astral Plane 26
    Astral Projection 26
    Astrology 27
    Athame 27
    Attunement 27
    Aura 27
    Avatar 28

Balefire	28
Bane	28
Banish	28
Besom	28
Between the Worlds	29
Bi-Location	29
Binding	29
Blast	29
Black Magic	29
Black Moon	30
Blessed Be	30
Blood of the Moon	30
Bolline	30
Book of Shadows	30
Burning Times	31
Cakes and Ales	31
Candles	31
Cardinal Points	31
Cape	32
Cauldron	32
Censer	32
Centering	32
Chakra	33
Chalice	33
Channeling	33
Chanting	33
Charge of the Goddess	34
Charge	34
Charms	34
Circle	34
Clairvoyance	34
Cleansing	35
Cone of Power	35
Conjuration	35
Consecrate	35
Corn Doll	35
Coven	36
Covenstead	36
Cowan	36
Crone	36
Crystal Elixir	36
Cross-Quarter Days	37

Crystal Ball	37
Curses	37
Dawning Down the Sun	37
Days of Power	37
Dedication	37
Degrees of Witchcraft	38
Deflection	38
Deity	38
Deosil	38
Divination	38
Dowsing	38
Drawing Down the Moon	39
Earth Power	39
Eke Name	39
Elder	39
Elements	39
Equinox	39
Esbat	40
Familiars	40
Five-Fold Kiss	40
Fluffy Bunny	40
Great Rite	40
Grimoire	40
Group Practitioner	41
Handfasting	41
High Priest or Priestess	41
Hiving Off	41
Incantation	41
Initiation	41
Intentions	41
Invoke	42
Lady and Lord	42
Left-Hand Path	42
Libation	42
Lunar Eclipse	42
Magical Alphabets	42
Magick	43
Maiden	43
Manifest	43
Merry Meet	43
Mother	43
Necromancy	43

Neophyte	44
Numerology	44
Occult	44
Omen	44
Pagan	44
Palm Reading	44
Pantheistic	45
Pantheon	45
Pendulum	45
Pentacle	45
Pentagram	45
Personal Power	46
Planes	46
Potion	46
Prana	46
Precognition	46
Projective Energy	46
Receptive Energy	47
Reincarnation	47
Right-Hand Path	47
Ritual	47
Rule of Three	47
Runes	48
Sabbats	48
Scourge	48
Scrying	48
Séance	48
Shadow Work	48
Sigils	49
Skyclad	49
Smudging	49
Solstice	49
Solar Eclipse	49
Solitary Practitioner	49
Spell	50
Spirits of the Stones	50
Spiritualism	50
Summerlands	50
Summoner	50
Talisman	50
Tarot Cards	51
The Craft	51

Transmutation 51
Triple Goddess 51
Undine 51
Vision Quest 51
Wand 52
Warding 52
Warlock 52
Wheel of the Year 52
White Magic 53
Wiccan Rede 53
Wiccaning 53
Widdershins 53
Witch 53
Witchcraft 54
Witches Ladder 54
Witching Hour 54
Zodiac 54

Chapter 3 *Wiccan Rites and Celebrations* 55

The Wheel of the Year 55
Wiccan Rites 58

Chapter 4 *Mesmerizing Magic* 60

Types of Witches 60
Tasks to Get Started 62

Chapter 5 *Crystal Magic* 65

History of Crystal Magic 65
Commonly Used Crystals 67
Crystal Systems 79
Preparations 80
Creating Crystal Magic 88

Chapter 6 *Beyond What Glimmers* 92
Conclusion 95
Description 96

TAROT FOR DUMMIES
Learn Tarot Reading Exercises, Tarot Card Meanings, Tarot Spreads, Increase Your Intuition and Master the Art of Tarot

Introduction 99

Part I *A History of Tarot* 101

    14th Century 101
    15th Century 101
    16th Century 102
    17th Century 103
    18th Century 104
    19th Century 105
    20th Century into Present Times 107
    The Use of Tarot Cards Today 109

Part II *Understanding and Finding Meaning In The Tarot Deck* 111

    The Minor Arcana 111
    The Major Arcana 136

Part III *Dealing and Interpreting The Tarot Deck* 149

    Basic Tarot Dealing and Reading 149
    Advanced Tarot Dealing and Reading 154
    Additional Notes About Methods for Dealing 173
    Reading People When Reading the Cards 174
    Go with Your Gut 178
    Developing Your Signature Style 180
    Preparing and Cleansing Your Cards 180

Part IV *Tarot In The Modern World* 183

    Who Still Uses Tarot? 183
    Handling Skepticism 186
    Tarot On TV- Handling Stereotypes and Pop Culture Misconceptions 188
    Building a Following 190
    Can Tarot Be a Viable Business? 192
    Preserving and Promoting Tarot for the Future 197

Conclusion 202
Description 204

WICCA CRYSTAL MAGIC

Learn Wiccan Beliefs, Rituals & Magic, and How to Use Wiccan Spells Using Crystals & Mineral Stones

Lisa Miller

INTRODUCTION

Thanks for purchasing *Wicca Crystal Magic*. Hopefully, it will give you all the information you need to start practicing Wicca. It should also answer any questions you have about Wicca answered. Whatever your reasons for wanting to read this book, I invite you to read it with an open mind so that you can seriously consider all the possibilities of Wicca. People have treated Wicca as something darker and scarier than what it is, so I've made every attempt to clarify the misconceptions that are commonly held and to show that Wicca is a unique but beautiful religion that is open to all kinds of people. No matter who you are, you can have a place in Wicca.

This book will teach you the fundamental ideas of Wicca and Wiccan crystal magic. This book is perfect for beginners who know nothing or next to nothing, but it can also be useful for people who know about Wicca but want to learn some of the details that you don't usually find with a basic search. While there are plenty of resources online, this book is unique because it compiles all the information you need to get started on Wicca into one book in a clear, concise, and fun manner.

Without further ado, enjoy this book, and let Wicca fill your life with some magic. By the end of this book, you should have a better understanding of what being Wiccan entails, and you'll know how to start practicing Wicca if you are so inclined.

CHAPTER 1
Introducing Wicca

What Is Wicca?

For those of you who may be unfamiliar with Wicca, it helps to have a brief introduction into what Wicca means before starting on your journey to becoming Wicca or learning more about it. Many people misunderstand what it means to be a Wiccan, which means that they don't even consider that it might be a good religion for them before dismissing it. The erroneous views of Wiccans often are because people hate what they cannot understand. Too often, people do not try to understand Wicca, which leads to all the misleading stereotypes and beliefs about Wicca that permeate Western cultures. The more you learn about Wicca, the easier it will be to see that it is just like any other religion in that it promotes morality and community. All that's different is its belief system.

Wicca is the most predominant form of paganism in the United States, and it is prevalent across the world as well. People often use the word paganism to refer to ancient polytheistic religions, but it is much more than that. In fact, paganism refers to any religion that is not Abrahamic. Abrahamic religions include Christianity, Judaism, and Islam. Pagan religions include Druidism, Hinduism, and, of course, Wicca. People use paganism as a derogatory word that means uncivilized because that's how Abrahamic people viewed the ancient religions when they came in and dominated religiously. They saw cultures that endorsed human sacrifice as well as other sacrifices, and they viewed them as wrong and ignorant. Modern pagan religions like Wicca are in no way associated with human sacrifice, but the early judgments still linger.

Unfortunately, because of the wrong associations linked to Paganism, there has not been a lot of academic work about Pagan religions, which means it is hard to have exact statistics about how many Pagans are in the world and what their common behaviors are. While Wiccans might not mind being more private, it does make it hard for their religion to spread and hard for people to share truthful ideas about Wicca. In the 1990s, there were increased academic movements that studied pagan faiths, but the research is still relatively new and far from mainstream. The increasing information that is becoming available about witchcraft is blossoming with the internet. Yet, even then, it is shocking how limited the information is about Wicca and other forms of paganism.

Wicca is a form of paganism, but it is important to clarify that it is not representative of what all types of paganism believe. Paganism does not always include witchcraft, but Wicca does include witchcraft. Wicca is its own religion that outsiders need to treat as such. Just because other pagan religions support immoral things or evil (though most don't) doesn't mean that Wicca also supports those things. Thus, it's essential to be aware of what religions really are before making snap judgments about them.

Wicca is a religion that commonly emphasizes two deities— the God and the Goddess. These deities have different aspects, which means that they take on various forms. Some versions of Wicca can have additional gods and be pantheistic, but that all depends on how you choose to practice and what you want to emphasize in your practice. Don't worry too much about that right now. To start, you can focus on the broad brushstrokes of Wicca. You can learn more about the details later.

Wicca centers itself around the moon cycles, which are called Esbats and are related to the Goddess. It also focuses on the sun cycles, which are related to the God and mark the Sabbats, which are the eight main festivals of Wicca. The celestial bodies, therefore, are essential to Wiccans because they represent the times when Wiccans are most potent, and they dictate when and how Wiccans practice their religion. Wiccans often strive to align their rituals with the cycles of the moon and the sun. By doing this, they form a link between the celestial and the natural. This link is a vital connection for any Wiccan to make.

The natural is one of the most critical parts of Wicca. Many Wiccan beliefs are rooted in maintaining harmony between Wiccans and the nature that surrounds them. Wiccans believe that everything in life has an energy and that even non-living things are essential because of the energy that they contain. Thus, utilizing entities like crystals and herbs can help Wiccans with their magic by providing energy and unique properties. To be a good Wiccan, you have to learn to respect the Earth and wisely use everything that is on it. Finding that harmony between what surrounds you and what is inside you is one of the most rewarding parts of Wicca.

While Wicca is one religion, there are many ways that you can practice it. Wiccans commonly use several branches, and some methods fall outside of the mainstream branches. Thus, it can be hard to pinpoint what Wicca is. Several words are often associated with Wicca— witchcraft, esotericism, occult, new age, polytheistic, magical. Because Wicca means so many things to many people, these words are just the start of all the things that Wicca can represent to its practitioners. When you are Wiccan, there is only so much you can learn from a book. The true meaning of Wicca becomes more apparent when you practice it and learn what it means to you.

Wicca is a unique religion that draws inspiration from several cultures. It is a relatively new religion, but its roots are ancient, and it strives to bring practices that have been deemed scientifically as "superstitious" or "mythical" back into fashion. The magic that Wicca practices isn't the kind that you know of magicians or from pop culture. Instead, it's magic that emphasizes the power of your mind to control your relationship with the world around you. Magic is real, but that doesn't mean it looks like how you think it should. Wicca is more than just a religion or witchcraft is a culmination of the two, and it is a beautiful spiritual force.

Thirteen Principles of Witchcraft

Thirteen principles drive Wiccan witchcraft among several Wiccan groups. While these beliefs can vary based on your branch of Wicca, they are seen as necessary in most branches or shape the foundation of most Wiccan religions. While no one thing is Wicca, these principles were created in 1974 to try to unify some of the Wiccan beliefs, and the Council made these laws of American Witches. You do not have to follow all of these based on how you practice, but they can give a good idea of what beliefs Wiccans find most important. They follow these rules along with the Wiccan Rede, which is that they should not harm others.

1. The seasons dictated by the moon distinguish Wiccans practice rituals and spells that help them become more aligned with the natural forces that drive life and these forces. The Wiccan holidays fall at the seasonal quarters and cross quarters. Everything that a Wiccan does centers around these forces, and they should drive themselves to channel their energy to reflect the forces around them and to celebrate the power that comes with those forces. The more Wiccans can be aware of the natural energies that surround them, the better able they will be to do spells and create more potent magic.

2. Wiccans recognize that they have a responsibility for the well-being of the environment because of their increased knowledge and love of nature. They strive to find balance with nature and protect it whenever they can. Wiccans do not want to harm the Earth. They want to help heal it and let it evolve as it needs to. They are not to neglect the sanctity of the Earth or anything on it because all things have energies that witches need to consider before doing anything. The health of Earth is vital to the health of the people on it, so it cannot be ignored by Wiccans.

3. Wiccans acknowledge that they have greater power than other people on Earth. They accept that some people will consider this power to be supernatural, but to Wiccans, this power is not supernatural. It is inherent within nature, and they have channeled it in their practices. They believe that anyone can bring magic into the world, but not everyone chooses to do so. The energies needed for magic are at each person's fingertips, and the joy of Wicca is knowing how to harness that power through the wisdom that has witches pass down through Wiccans via covens and oral histories.

4. Wiccans also embrace the polarity of the universe. There is a balance between the masculine and the feminine, and this balance gives Wiccans more power when they acknowledge it. Wiccans can be more creative when they manifest the

polarity of the universe. Interaction between the masculine and the feminine embrace this polarity and allow for more significant witchcraft. Neither masculinity nor femininity is superior to the other, which is one of the ways that Wicca promotes equality among people rather than trying to divide people. Wiccans should embrace both polarities for ideal results. This tenet also encourages the use of sex for not only a source of energy but a manner for obtaining pleasure and a symbol for life being personified.

5. Wiccans do not prioritize one world over the other. They recognize that there are both inner and outer worlds that include the unconscious. The various planes are not to be deemed as more important than one another because they are all paramount in the well-being of a Wiccan. The ability to create communication between the dimensions is the heart of magic and other spiritual encounters that are driven by the Wiccan religion. Allowing the other planes to exist and paying attention to them allows Wiccans to do things that other humans cannot do because they close their minds off to spiritual ideas and ignore the other planes that they cannot see.

6. Wiccans are against any hierarchy that creates authoritarian behavior, but they do honor people who are more advanced in Wicca and who pass on the traditions and keep it alive. Wiccans respect those who came before, but they can see beyond the hierarchy when they need and embrace individuality. Wicca is not like becoming a certain person. It is a way to practice one's uniqueness within a group setting. Thus, the insight of the elders should be valued, but it should not be the sole information that practitioners use to make their decisions.

7. Wiccans view knowledge, their religion, and magick as enmeshed. These three properties are a part of life, and Wiccans must incorporate all three into their behaviors. The art of witchcraft is a worldview that Wiccans share, and people cannot dissect this art while remaining Wiccan. Wicca is practiced in diverse ways, but both witchcraft and religion and the wisdom that go into them are linked in ways

that make them inseparable. Learn as much as you can about these three areas and look at them holistically to embrace the teachings of Wicca.

8. Wiccans believe that just because you use the title "witch" does not mean that you are a witch, nor does your family line alone make you a witch. It doesn't matter if you call yourself a witch or are in a family that has had generations of witches. Even those who are of the highest degrees of witchcraft are not witches if they do not embrace the energies around them. Wiccan witches must learn to balance all the energies and use them for functional purposes. To be a true witch requires control. Wiccans have learned how to control the forces within and without themselves, and they can do so with wisdom and morality.

9. Wiccans have faith in their abilities to learn about the universe and to give meaning to it through their craft. They believe that by doing magic and practicing their religion that they will have a better consciousness about commonly unknown things. They will become aware of parts of the universe that the average person never becomes aware of. This awareness will lead to fulfillment in the Wiccan's life, but this awareness is never finite. There are always more opportunities to raise awareness about the world and to become wiser. There will never be a day when a Wiccan is too smart or has a consciousness about everything. Being on Earth means that Wiccans have something left to learn.

10. Wiccans only feel resentment towards other religions such as Christianity because of those religions claiming that they are the only religions that will provide salvation and good things. Wiccans do not like the view that there is just one way to find personal solace and freedom. Unfortunately, many prevalent religions in the west preach that their way is the only way, which is discordant with Wiccan philosophy. Wiccans do not hate Christian religion in and of itself, so they do not claim to be the only way, and they do not try to prevent people from practicing their religions or look down upon those people for having different religions.

11. Wiccans in America have determined that they do not need to worry about the history of witchcraft or the origins of specific terms because those ideas do not help them move forward. They instead want to focus on the now and what the future will bring for Wiccans. Debating about what once was is a waste of time and energy because it will not bring harmony into their lives. Instead, Wiccans choose to focus on things that will bring them inner and outer peace presently. The past contains lots of good information, but you shouldn't treat the past with bitterness and over-attention because that will do you no good.

12. Wiccans do not believe that there is absolute evil, nor do they accept embracing this evil and using it in acts of witchcraft. Accordingly, they do not believe in Satan, and they indeed do not worship him. They acknowledge the right of others to worship the devil if that is what they think is right, but that can never be a Wiccan practice. Wiccans do not want to harm others in their practices. They are okay with witches practicing to get personal gain, but that personal gain can not be the expense of other people. Wiccans follow the Wiccan Rede, which is a law that insists that they don't hurt other people.

13. Wiccans believe that they should use nature to find fulfillment and to search for things that will give them health and well-being. They believe that all that they need to better themselves is surrounding them. All they need to do is focus their energies and find ways to balance themselves and their energies with the ones that are in nature. Wicca is a matter of finding harmony, which will promote the inner and outer tranquility that Wiccans strive to achieve. The universe has so much to offer, but most people do not embrace what they cannot see, so they miss out on many skills and acts that could make them feel more connected to their surroundings and themselves.

While the Council of American witches does not exist anymore, there are many sects of American Wiccans and witches that still use these fundamental doctrines to guide their practices. Further, many Wiccans across the world have similar tenets even if branches of Wicca have not worded them as such. Thus, these thirteen principles, whether you choose to use them or not, give you a better idea of what Wicca is as a whole and the general parameters that Wiccans follow.

History of Wicca

Wicca is a religion that you can predominantly find in the Western world. While Wicca has roots in the Celtic world and with other pre-Christian religions, Wicca was more heavily motivated by Victorian influences. During Victorian times, people would create societies in which they would practice magic in secret. At that time, witchcraft was criminal, but these groups persevered nevertheless and passed on their writings to the next generation. While it would be years before Wicca became fully formed, the writings and work of the Victorians would fuel the witches who would come years later. Thinkers like Margaret Murray, the "Grandmother of Wicca," who worked in the 1920s, and Aleister Crowley, who started occult work in 1914, were essential figures who predated the emergence of modern Wicca but were nevertheless influential in its creation.

There are forms of Wicca that came before, but the founder of modern is considered by Wiccans to be Gerald Brosseau Gardner. Gardner lived in Asia for a spell as a British civil servant, and he began to discover new things about himself and the world while he was in Asia. During his time in Asia, Gardner started to study the occult, which led to him organizing a religion around the information he unveiled. Much of what he learned was from sources like Aleister Crowley, a significant name in the world of the occult who was a witch during Victorian times. When he finished his service in Asia, Gardner returned to Britain just before WWII commenced. When he returned, he used esoteric knowledge from writings to begin interacting with occult groups that had already started in England. Doreen Valiente assisted Gardner in bringing his ideas to life and forming the Wiccan religion that we know today.

It was hard being Wiccan in early times. Until 1951, the United Kingdom still had laws that banned witchcraft, so it wasn't until those laws went away that Gardner was able to publish his seminal

1954 work, *Witchcraft Today*. This book was one of several that brought attention to Wicca and spread the ideas of the religion. At that time, he also started his own coven. The members of his new coven were central parts of the Wiccan development process, and they helped Gardner create a foundation for Wicca that would be better for more types of people.

Gardner himself did not call his religion Wicca, but the practice became called that because the people who practiced the religion were often titled, "the Wicca." It wasn't until after Gardner died in 1964 that Wicca became the title of the faith officially. The word is known to mean "wise people," which refers to the wisdom of other plans and spiritual realms that Wicca can reach through their practice of Wicca. When Gardner died, Wicca began to spread even more, and it reached far beyond Europe, where it had originated. Wicca blossomed in ways that Gardner probably didn't expect.

Throughout the 1960s, Wicca began to grow in popularity, and it spread to other countries like the United States. In the United States, Wicca, with its emphasis on nature and its forward-thinking views on femininity, echoed many of the movements already happening in the United States. For many people, it was a comfort during an incredibly turbulent decade. Wicca allowed people to engage in spiritual practices without having to be part of restrictive, well-established religions. Free-spirited people flocked to Wicca, and they began the Craft with eagerness. Wicca was something new and exciting, and it shattered the ideal of conformity that had been the status quo in the 1950s.

By the 1980s, Wicca had 50,000 practitioners in the world, mostly in Europe and the United States. The eighties brought new recognition to Wicca, and people began to see that it was a legitimate religion. In 1984, in the case of Dettmer v. Landon, the United States recognized that Wicca is classified as a religion. Before Dettmer v. Landon, authorities had said that Wicca was not a religion because it had occult activities; however, the case solidified that because it was common practice and followed all qualifications to be a religion that it had to be considered a religion. The decision to label Wicca an official religion was a victorious decision for witches everywhere, some of whom still didn't get the recognition they deserved, or they faced discrimination.

Wicca doesn't have a hierarchical structure like many religions, so while Gardner was important, he was not the only notable figure in the world of Wicca. Many Wiccans followed Gardner's teachings, but other people found unique ways to practice Wicca. As Wicca grew, it began to branch off into a new version of itself. Not all practitioners wanted to use Gardernarian practicers. Alexander Sanders was one of the earliest sects of Wicca to branch off. His practice eventually branched off into Dianic Wicca. Some of these Wiccans did not like the use of the word "witch," and they chose not to use that term even though they were still practicing witchcraft. Certain groups continued to practice in the nude, which was called traditionalist because practicing in the nude was practiced by witches before even Gardner was around. Others wore robes or just their regular clothes. Wiccans began practicing in whole new ways, but Gardner was still considered the founder of all things Wicca. Other leaders just took Gardner's ideas and tweaked them to match their needs as Wiccans. Thus, Wicca allows for considerable flexibility in its practices, and anyone can find a sect of Wicca that matches their needs and beliefs.

Presently, there are up to one and a half million Wiccans around the world. In the United States, there are 300,000 Wiccans, and Wiccans are the biggest group of neo-pagan faiths in the country. The breakdown of branches of Wiccans is less clear because there could be hundreds of types of Wiccans, which makes it hard to keep track of all the branches that have arisen since Gardner's time. Nevertheless, it is obvious that Wicca has become an important religion, and it is something that people continue to learn and join.

Wicca is the most prominent religion related to witchcraft, and it is a safe-haven for many people who are looking to belong and lay down spiritual roots. People practice it in many different ways, but no matter how you practice Wicca, it helps connect you to yourself and the world around you. Plus, it allows you to create some magic that will help you improve your life. What's not to like?

What Wicca and Wiccans Are Not

There are many erroneous views of what Wicca is out there. These views make Wicca seem like it is malevolent or scary. Unfortunately, in the 1980s, Satanic Panic arose, and it caused people to question all things that weren't Christian. They became certain that Satan was taking over society through occult behaviors and occultism. This led to incidents like the satanic ritual abuse, which were wrongful allegations against childcare centers that were false but sprung up in the eighties because of fears of the devil. Wicca is lumped in with Satanism, and people became fearful of it, but Wicca is not something that anyone should be scared of, and through debunking the myths around it, you'll be able to see that Wicca and Wiccans aren't weird and scary.

Wicca is not weird contrary to popular belief. Because Wiccans use magic, people often think that Wiccans are weird and mysterious, but that couldn't be farther from the truth. Wiccans aren't stranger than any other person. They have different beliefs that aren't often understood by Western culture, but their views are as reasonable as any other religion. Wiccans should not be judged by people who don't even realize what they are trying to do through their spiritual practices. Admittedly, there are some strange Wiccans, but they are not inherently odd because of their weirdness (nor is weirdness a bad thing)!

Wicca is not interchangeable with the witchcraft. While Wiccans practice witchcraft, there are lots of types of witchcraft that do not fall under the Wiccan branch, and some of those other practices are not religious like Wicca is. Other religions use witchcraft, but don't practice Wicca. Thus, Wiccans and witches aren't interchangeable words. You can call a Wiccan a witch (for most of the branches), but you cannot call all witches Wiccans. Some witches do not practice religion at all, and so to associate them with Wicca would not be like calling every Christian a Catholic.

Wicca is not devil worship. The link between Wicca and Satanism is entirely unfounded. Wicca is not an Abrahamic religion, which means that Wiccans don't even believe in the devil. In the Wiccan religion, there is no view of absolute evil, so no figure like Satan exists. Thus, any associations that have been made between Satan and Wiccans are not well-researched and are not accurately linked conclusions.

Further, people who call them Satanists *and* Wiccans may not understand what Wicca is either and are likely not real practitioners. If you ever hear that Wicca equals satanism, you are hearing the perpetuation of people vilifying what they don't know. In these cases, people make judgments without any understanding of what is factual. The more these judgments spread, the harder it is for people to understand Wicca.

Wicca is not evil. Just like Wicca isn't satanism, it also isn't evil. The Wiccan Rede ensures that Wiccan does not use their magic for evil. Evil acts do a Wiccan no good, so there's no reason to be afraid that a Wiccan is going to try to destroy the world or hurt other people. Wiccans respect the world inherently, so they will value all the energies that the Earth has rather than trying to hurt it. Wiccans prioritize acts that help themselves and the community without resorting to evil deeds. Morality is essential in Wicca, just as it is in other religions.

Wicca does not encourage harming others to better oneself. Again, the Wiccan Rede prohibits Wiccans from hurting others to benefit themselves. Of course, that doesn't mean that a Wiccan will never use their magic for immoral purposes, but when they do harmful acts, they *are* breaking the values that Wicca holds dear. Wicca is all about creating positive forces and allowing the bad ones to be improved, so to harm others is to harm the mission of creating balance. When you harm others, you break the balance and compromise the well-being of your spiritual self.

Wicca is not an ancient religion. While Wicca has ancient roots, people created it in the twentieth century, so it is not ancient in its practices. It borrows a lot from ancient and Victorian times, but it has embraced modern principles. Accordingly, it does not encourage some more uncivilized behaviors like human sacrifice. Further, it reflects current cultures in ways that older religions don't because it was born with modern challenges and beliefs in mind. Thus, it furthers ideas such as feminism and environmentalism.

Wicca is not a "fake" religion. Governments have recognized it throughout the world as a valid religion rather than one that has been fabricated. Let me emphasize: Wicca is real, and it is legitimate, so do not doubt that even if you don't want to take part in it.

Wiccans don't make animal sacrifices. They respect the energies of animals, and they don't need to kill them in rituals. There may be rare Wiccans who work outside of regular Wiccan circles who use such practices, but an animal (or especially human) sacrifice is not encouraged. It does not help Wiccans balance their power.

Wiccans aren't hypersexual. While Wiccans may be more sexually open and are welcoming of all types of people, that does not mean that Wiccans like to have orgies. Being incredibly sexual isn't inherently sexual. Some Wiccans do practice naked, but even then, their nudity is a way of doing better magic and worshipping rather than something sexual in nature.

Wiccans practice magic, but they aren't like the witches you see in pop culture phenomena like *Sabrina the Teenage Witch* or *Harry Potter*. Witches can point at something and have sparks zap out of their fingers. They can't have one thought and change a person into a zoo animal. Witches do have power, but their influence is less glamorous than it appears in movies and other pop culture.

Wiccans are much more than many people give them credit for being. They are not all the same, and Wiccans are free to take some liberties with their practices because Wicca is not as rigid as many other religions, which is why it is so appealing to those who practice it.

What Wiccans and Wicca Are

More important than what Wicca isn't and who Wiccans aren't is what Wicca is and who Wiccans aren't. It is the things that define Wicca and Wiccans that make it stand out from all else.

Wicca is inviting. One of the best parts of Wicca is that it is open to people of all genders, races, and sexualities. No matter who you are, there is a place in the Wiccan community for you. Wicca allows you to be yourself within a community of people who may not be accepted elsewhere. Witchcraft has long been something that is done for outsiders, and Wicca is a religion that continues that practice while adding additional spiritual values that help guide people and give them structure. Wicca does not close its doors to people who are unaccepted elsewhere. It is open to all who want to live by its tenets.

Wicca is driven by good. At its core, it wants to create a world and a self that it is better. Wicca wants to follow the right-hand path. It wants to further the goodness of the world because that is what will lead to spiritual health. In Wicca, no one benefits from doing bad. Bad deeds may fulfill temporary wants, but they will not be good for a person in the long run. Wiccans know that following the Wiccan Rede is the wise thing to do, and they know that while their magic gives them power, it must be used responsibly or their bad deeds will come back upon them three times over.

Wicca is magical. Wicca embraces spells, incantations, divining, and so much more. It uses magic as part of its rituals, so when you are Wiccan, magic is automatically a part of your daily life. It becomes one of the most important facets of yourself, and the magic helps you deepen your faith. With magic, you can expand your abilities, and those abilities allow you to better serve your coven. They show you the good in the world, and they give you the promise of balance.

Wicca is a community. Wicca allows you to connect with likeminded people who also want to create magic. It gives you something bigger to believe in, and it allows you to see the world beyond yourself. Wiccans can find groups that welcome them and make them feel safe. While you don't need to interact with other Wiccans, communication with people who share your faith is incredibly rewarding and it helps you grow as a person. When you can share spiritual experiences, you have more power, and you have a group of people you know will always support you and be there to guide you.

Wiccans are individuals, and they love to use this individuality in their religion. They are unique people even when they are a part of a coven. They make their own decisions and they value nonconformity. The Wiccan faith gives them guidelines, but it also gives them plenty of chances to be themselves and to embrace what makes them special. Wiccans are diverse, and that's what makes the Wiccan community so wonderful. No two Wiccans look the same; yet, they are just as welcome in the Wiccan community. Wiccans are boldy themselves, and that's pretty admirable.

Branches of Wicca

There are several branches of Wicca that can be found across the world. While the distinctions aren't all that important because of how flexible Wicca is and how it can be personalized to your needs, it may help to find a branch that appeals to you and that best meets your individual needs. This list of branches is not exhaustive, but it gives you a good idea of what kind of Wiccans are out there. Likely, there are hundreds of branches of Wicca that can be found. Therefore, there is a group for everyone. Don't feel a need to label yourself any particular way when you first get started. It can take some time before you realize what you want from your experience with Wicca. Let your process happen organically rather than trying to force anything.

Alexandrian

The Alexandrian Wiccans tend to be less restrictive and allow members greater liberty. This group was formed by Alexander Sanders with the help of Maxine, his wife. This group is very closely related to the Gardnerian group, but they are allowed more freedom with worshipping deities outside of the traditional Wiccan ones, and they have more options when it comes to the rituals. Alexandrians, for example, encourage followers to work in the nude because being naked is related to freedom, but they do not have to.

In this tradition, they still use two deities, but they primarily use the aspects of the Horned God and the Mother Goddess as the primary forms of the deities. This practice can be found across the world, and it is one of the more common traditions of Wicca. It is still fairly traditional even though it is less traditional than Gardnerian Wicca. Thus, this type of Wicca is perfect for anyone who likes Gardnerian Wicca but wants less rigidity in how they practice.

Caledonii

Caledonii Wiccans practice their Wicca based on the religious origins of tribes in Scotland that were called the Caledonii by the Romans. This is a Celtic inspired religion that is part of Caledonii, but it is a subgroup. The Caledonii believe in being welcoming to people and embracing diversity. There are three main branches of the Caledonia Grande Tradition: Caledonii Druidic Order, Celtic Wicca, and Caledonii Federation. There are also more minor branches such as the Culdee Church of Celtic Christianity. All these religions have Caledonia roots, but they are not all Wiccan, so keep that in mind as you do more research.

Celtic

Celtic Wiccans incorporate Celtic traditions into their worship. Celtic people were originally found in areas such as the United Kingdom, Ireland, and France before the Christians took over. The Celtic festivals are the basis for the festivals that Wiccans in all branches celebrate today. The festivals have been renamed to better reflect Wiccan tradition, but for Celtic Wiccans, they use the old Celtic names. Celtic Wiccans also learn about Celtic mythology, which has additional gods and goddesses as well as stories of other beings such as the fae. Celtic Wiccans are very different from traditional Wiccans, but these groups are perfect for those who wish to celebrate both Celtic and Wiccan cultures.

Dianic

Dianic Wiccans are considered to be especially feminist witches. This tradition was created based on the works of an author, Zsuzsanna Budapest. The Dianic covens began in the United States in the 1970s, and it spread throughout the decade. Dianic covens emphasize the role of the Goddess and this version of Wicca is, therefore, monotheistic in many cases. They celebrate different versions of the Goddess, but all these versions are still just one deity. They also often only have women as members of the coven. Dianic groups make women feel safe gathering and practicing their witchcraft with men being there to enforce patriarchal patterns. Some Dianic witches have branched off from the all-female groups, and they encourage all genders to enter their groups, and they acknowledge the God as a secondary figure to the Goddess. Thus, in Dianic groups, the most important distinction is the worship of the goddess above all else.

Eclectic

Eclectic is probably the most common branch of Wicca, but it is hard to tell the exact numbers of who is doing what kind of Wicca. Eclectic Wicca describes all versions of Wicca that are less rigid and don't make followers go down a certain path. Eclectic Wiccans are free to determine which deities they want to worship and even what holidays they want to celebrate. They make their own traditions. Eclectic witchcraft can be done in solitary or in covens, depending on what the individual Wiccan wants. This version of Wicca gives you the most options to define your own faith. It can be helpful to start your journey out here as you figure out what you want to get out of Wicca and how you want to practice it.

Gardnerian

This branch of Wicca is the original branch, and it is named after Gerald Gardner. Because this branch steps back to the original group of Wiccans, they tend to emphasize traditional beliefs, and they are more inflexible when it comes to how they practice. They often do their work in the nude, and their covens are run by High Priestesses. The hierarchy of the coven is more profound in this tradition than it is in other traditions. Gardnerians also tend to be highly secretive, preferring to keep to themselves. While Gardnerian witches have to follow more rules and stay true to the origins of Wicca, this rigidity is helpful for some witches who need more structure.

In the Gardnerian branch of Wicca, there are three degrees of witchcraft. The first marks when someone has been dedicated and initiated into a coven. The second degree marks when a witch has moved beyond fundamental witchcraft and has grown into the coven. The third degree is when members rise in ranks through the coven and have leadership roles. A "fourth" degree is when members become the High Priest or High Priestess, which is the highest rank in a coven. When they are at the third-degree, practitioners may start their own coven to allow growth in the Wiccan faith.

Gardnerians tend to be more secretive than other branches, and they have intricate rituals that more modern branches don't always have. This sect of Wicca is found across the world, and it is popular because it is the original branch of Wicca. Though, many Wiccans like to have less structure in their practice of Wicca.

Georgian

George Patterson created his own branch of Wicca. He encouraged his followers to be unique and to embrace their own paths. Much of what he teaches follows Alexandrian principles, but Georgian Wicca is even more laid-back, so it allows more liberty with how you practice it. Patterson would tell followers to do what works and to not do what doesn't work. While Georgian is one of the significant branches of Wicca, it is quite eclectic, and it retains structure while also allowing lots of flexibility. Many practitioners like this style of Wicca because it remains an individualistic whole, still being an organized religion. In Georgian Wicca, you can and should be your unique self.

Hellenic

Hellenic Wiccans incorporate Greek beliefs into their Wicca. It is a merging of the traditional Wicca as well as the ancient Greek religion. Some of the Greek gods that Hellenic Wiccans include are Zeus, Poseidon, Hera, and Apollo, as well as others. The Greek pantheon is open to Hellenic Wiccans to worship and invoke in spells. If you are interested in Greek mythology, you might adore this version of Wicca!

Seax

Seax is a style of Wicca that encourages a more solitary approach to the religion. It was founded by Raymond Buckland, who was appalled when he saw corruption within covens. He didn't like the way the hierarchy could cause weird power dynamics that took away from the religion, so he started a branch of his own that would be fitting to people who wanted the option to practice Wicca by themselves. This practice often uses some Germanic deities such as Freya. Further, it uses runes more heavily than other sects of Wicca. Seax is the most individualistic group of Wiccans beyond those who don't organize in these groups at all.

Core Beliefs

Certain core beliefs drive Wiccans to act the way that they do. These core beliefs are the universal parts of the Wiccan religion, and they make Wiccan distinct from other pagan religions. These beliefs bond Wiccans everywhere with a shared interest in values and parts of the world that are as said to matter the most. If you are interested in or feel drawn to the following beliefs, Wicca may be an ideal path for you, and it may help you balance your physical and spiritual selves. Even if they don't appeal to you right now, if you give Wicca a try, you might be able to learn and grow into these beliefs.

Nature is an important part of the Wiccan belief system. As you know, the natural world is full of energy that Wiccans use to their advantage. Magic, of course, is another crucial part of Wicca. Magic is used to varying degrees by Wiccans, but it is always part of a Coven's rituals. Like any religion, Wicca has rituals that it uses to worship the gods and to spiritually grow. These rituals connect the Wiccan community.

Wiccans believe in balance. They think that through their practices they can promote the balance in all areas of themselves. They believe that there is much more than just the physical self and that a person is made up of many parts that balance their physical, emotional, and spiritual parts. They believe in psychic energies and the ability to foretell the future as well as shape it through spells.

The belief in the God and the Goddess as the two prominent deities is one of the most important beliefs of Wicca across all branches, and these are so important that you could write a book just on the deities! These deities represent polarity in the world as they are both masculine and feminine and sun and moon. Both deities have different aspects that are various forms that they take to represent various things.

Wiccans believe in these ideas and so much more that you'll learn throughout this book. At their core, Wiccans want to find tranquility in their lives, and they want to manage the chaos that comes from being alive. They can manage this chaos by worshipping the deities, practicing magic, respecting the earth and everything on it, and allowing themselves to remain balanced even in the face of chaos.

CHAPTER 2
Terms To Know

There are many terms that it helps to know before diving into Wicca more seriously. Whenever you need clarification on a term, you can check back to this list for reference. Don't feel like you have to memorize all of these terms right now (that would be overwhelming). Instead, familiarize yourself with them and build upon your knowledge of these terms as you start going deeper into Wicca.

Absent Healing

This is a method of transferring positive energy to a sick person, but in this process, the healer is not with the sick person when the healing commences. This kind of healing refers to both healing of the mind, the soul, or the body.

Acolyte

An acolyte is a person in a coven who is new to witchcraft. This term often refers to the lowest rank of a Wiccan. Acolytes have only started their journey, but they have plenty of room to grow and learn from elders of their coven so that they can rise through the ranks.

Adept

This term refers to a witch who is incredibly talented in a certain form of magic. Usually, this term is used to describe people who have been Wiccan for a long time and have practiced extensively. It can be used by witches who are not Wiccan as well, but it is primarily a Wiccan term.

Akasha

Akasha is the fifth element after water, air, fire, and earth. It represents spiritual energy that is present on the earth, and it is part of all the other elements. Thus, it is a special and all-consuming element that can be found anywhere you look if you make the effort to sense it.

Akashic Records

Akashic Records are the histories of people's past lives as well as tons of other knowledge. They are found within astral planes, so they cannot be seen without astral travel. Some practitioners also believe that these records are prophetic and have secrets about the future as well.

Altar

An altar is an important space for Wiccans. It is where artifacts for worship are kept, and it is a focal point for ritual, sacred practices. Altars can contain various elements, but you can find these in the homes of witches, and they are personalized based on the individual witch's expertise. Usually, they are built to be elevated, but they may also be found on the ground. Some items that may be found on an altar include chalices, cauldrons, or candles.

Anima

Anima is the feminine parts of a man that are kept within his psyche. In Wicca, the balance between masculine and feminine energies is important, making the religion one that values both the power of males and females, which is one of the most special elements of the religion.

Amulet

An amulet is often found as a piece of jewelry, and it is a charm that witches will keep with them for better luck and protection. This item is made by humans, and it can be made sacred by the witch who wears it or other witches.

Animism

Animism means that people give souls to inanimate things. Wiccans believe that everything has energies that they can channel and use for spells, which is why Wiccans have great respect for the natural world and everything on Earth. Those who agree with animism think that everything on earth has a unique spirit. Thus, even things like rocks have energies that need to be respected.

Ankh

Ankh refers to a cross that has a circle on the top. This cross is of Egyptian origin, but some Wiccans use it in their practices.

An-shet

An-shet is a word that is used by some to describe a wand. Use whatever terminology that you feel most comfortable with or that your coven encourages.

Apprentice

Apprentice is another term that is sometimes used to describe a beginner witch. The terminology that is used for a beginner will vary based on the other Wiccans that you associate with and the type of Wicca that you practice. Apprentices often get special attention from those with higher ranks and get hands-on help with their witchcraft.

Aspects

Aspects refer to the deities in their other forms or personas. The Goddess, for example, often takes on three forms— the maid, the mother, and the crone. Those three parts all make up the same deity, but they are used to represent different parts of the overarching deity. The three parts of the female deity represent the various stages of life that women go through.

Asperger

An asperger is a grouping of several herbs (or another object that can let water through) that have been brought together to use for purification. This can be used either before or after a ritual. Water is put through the asperger during the purification, and the water can be put on people or things.

Astral Body

An astral body is a person within, the spiritual part of you, who travels when you astral project. It is the psychic version of your body. It can't be seen in the physical plane, but you can see it and others can see it in the astral realm.

Astral Plane

An astral plane is also known as an astral realm or word. It is a plane of existence separate from the one that you physically exist in. You cannot see the astral plane when you go about your normal life. You cannot put the astral plane into your GPS and expect to get there. While it can be hard to get to an astral plane, especially when you first attempt to, it is not impossible. Many witches can get there with practice. The astral plane is appealing to witches and Wiccans because it allows people to have a consciousness that they cannot reach in the regular realm of existence. In the astral plane, you can push boundaries that your physical body normally prevents you from getting near, which is why the astral plane can allow you to accomplish greater things and get in touch with your spirituality.

Astral Projection

Astral projection is the process you use to reach the astral plane. It means that you can separate your astral body from your physical body and project yourself to new places. This is often also considered an out of body experience. This process opens up your eyes to new experiences, and it is one of the most exciting adventures you can go on. It's like traveling without having to leave the comfort of your home. It does take practice to learn how to do this skill, but it is a wonderful process that can help you see beyond the physical plane.

Astrology

Astrology is a metaphysical science that explores the meaning of the celestial bodies and how their alignments can help people channel their energies to create witchcraft and how those celestial bodies can predict the future. Astrology uses bodies, including the sun, the stars, and the moon, to determine what will happen and how people should act. The zodiac is one of the most common astrological ideas, and it used the alignment of the celestial bodies to assign birth charts that dictate how people behave. Some Wiccans pay special attention to astrology, and for all Wiccans, the cycle of the moon is important because it marks the major Wiccan festivals. Witches often align their spells to the phases of the moon to ensure they are using their power as well as they can be. You probably already know your astrological sign, but astrology is much more than just your zodiac sign and takes extensive study.

Athame

An athame is a double-edged dagger that usually has a black handle. It is a knife that is mostly used for rituals rather than for cutting things. When this dagger is put into a chalice, it represents the joining of masculine and feminine. The chalice represents the female energy while the athame represents the masculine because it is a phallic symbol. You can also use this tool to create circles for witchcraft.

Attunement

Attunement refers to any activity that aligns the inner parts of yourself. When you are attuned, you feel calmer and it is a harmonious state.

Aura

Aura refers to an energy that is invisible to many people but can be seen by Wiccans and other witches when they train themselves to see it. Auras are glows that form around people, and these glows reflect the personalities and vibes of the people who the auras surround. The aura will be made up of different colors in different locations around the person. The different areas of humans that the aura reflects are chakras.

Avatar

An avatar is a soul that has a higher status and returns to a body with a lower status to teach less advanced people. This can be seen in Christianity through Jesus, and it can be seen in Hinduism through Buddha, but it is also sometimes applied in Wiccan practices as well. This can also be referred to as a Bodhisattva.

Balefire

A balefire is fundamentally a bonfire that Wiccans use for their festivals. These fires are mostly used on the festivals of Yule, Midsummer, and Beltane, but they can also be used to help with magic on non-holidays and other holidays than the ones listed.

Bane

A bane is something that is evil and is a force that tries to destroy things. Banes will make your life more difficult. Something that is a bane can be banished by a coven or individual witches.

Banish

Banish means to send away bad energies or entities via magic. Wiccans sometimes must combat harmful forces by banishing them. Banishment can be done as a group or as individuals. Wiccans banish things by using banishing rituals, which can take a variety of forms.

Besom

A besom is a broomstick that is used for magic. Brooms in pop culture are often said to be something that witches ride. You should not try to fly on your brooms. You'll end up hurting yourself, but you can use brooms to brush away negative energy and clear away any bad luck. Many witches favor wooden brooms because they more closely look like a tree and are closer to nature, but whatever broom you have will do.

Between the Worlds

This is a concept related to the circle that Wiccans use in many rituals. It is the idea that when in the Wiccan Circle, you are between the physical and the spiritual worlds. Thus, you can associate with those who are in the spirit world.

Bi-Location

This is a term that means seeing a person physically at the same time that others see their astral body.

Binding

Binding is using magic to inhibit either a person or a thing. When you do a binding spell, you commonly use ropes or other objects that you can tie into knots. Binding often requires learning about different knots and their purposes. Mostly, this is used to prevent a person from either hurting themselves or hurting others.

Blast

To blast someone is to curse them.

Black Magic

Black magic is the kind of magic that Wiccans do not permit. It is magic that is used to harm other people or trick them. It is often called "the left-hand path," and it is a path of evil. The witches who practice black magic are selfish and evil. If you want to use black magic, which I hope you don't, Wicca is not for you. Further, black magic is dangerous, so practitioners who use it put themselves at risk.

Black Moon

A black moon refers to an extra new moon in a month. Sometimes, it can also mean that a full or new moon is missing in a month. The black moon is a time when Wiccans have more power, so it is a time when Wiccans tend to do more spells and rituals. As a powerful time for witches, black moons can be incredibly exciting.

Blessed Be

Blessed be is a multipurpose phrase that Wiccans can use to greet and say goodbye to one another. They may also use it as a response in rituals. It is meant to remind Wiccans that they are surrounded by sacred things. When they say it, Wiccans use the three-syllable pronunciation.

Blood of the Moon

Blood of the moon is a term used to describe when a female has the most power. Often, this time aligns with a woman's menstrual cycle, which is why they call it the blood of the moon. Some witches align their spells with their menstrual cycle to channel their energy. Sometimes, this is only used when the woman's menstruation happens on the full or new moon. Of course, this term only is relevant for witches that have a menstrual cycle.

Bolline

The bolline is a knife with a white handle that is used for cutting. It is often used for herbs and inscriptions. Most Wiccans do not use this knife when they are not in the Wiccan Circle.

Book of Shadows

A book of shadows falls under the umbrella of the term grimoire. In its essence, it is a witch's diary. Wiccans use these books to keep track of their spells and write down incantations, rituals, and recipes. They log their experiences and jot down information that they think is most important. A book of shadows guides a witch and allows them to look back on all the work they have done. Your Book of Shadows doesn't have to be anything fancy, but you can buy some really nice journals that would do the trick. While some witches follow the practice of burning books of burning or otherwise destroying books of shadows when other witches die, some switches pass their books down to their loved ones to guide them. Though, often, traditions are passed down orally. The book of shadows got its name from the burning times when witches had to practice in the shadows to avoid being persecuted.

Burning Times

This term is a reference to when witches were killed for practicing witchcraft. It specifically refers to when the Catholic church killed pagans for their beliefs during the Inquisition and Reformation. Witches were burned in some areas, but they were hanged in others. Witches do not face the persecution that they once did, fortunately, but burning times is a reminder of the bad that can happen when witches are unfairly vilified.

Cakes and Ales

This term refers to a meal that is had at the end of a Wiccan ritual. It is often shared with the gods and goddesses.

Candles

You probably are familiar with burning candles for the lovely smell that they can have, but they are so much more than that to Wiccans. Wiccans often use candles and wax in their rituals. Differently colored candles have unique meanings, and they are used for distinct rituals based on those meanings. Frequently, rituals are commenced and ended with lighting and blowing out the candle. The candles usually are consecrated by witches, and they can be made of herbs or symbols can be carved into them.

Cardinal Points

Cardinal points are the directions north, south, east, and west. Pointing things in different directions can have different meanings during a ritual. In some traditions, the north is represented by green candles. South is represented by red, east is represented by yellow, and the west is represented by blue. In any case, the cardinal points are used to draw the Wiccan Circle, which is made based on the cardinal points.

Cape

A cape is often used for witches to better use their power. These capes will often be embroidered with special symbols, and they were only worn in the presence of the deities. Wiccans take them off when they are outside of their sacred spaces. Not all Wiccan wear capes, but some may choose to do so.

Cauldron

A cauldron is one of the tools that most people already associate with witchcraft. Cauldrons are used for several purposes, and they are most often made of iron, but you can use a regular pot that you already have in your house if you'd rather. The point is to be able to make good spells and potions, so if you don't have money to spare, don't worry about what your cauldron looks like because the quality of your magic is more important than your equipment. Cauldrons often represent being well-fed, both physically and emotionally. They also are a symbol of the Goddess' womb. Thus, they are used for potions and scrying that ensure the well-being of Wiccans.

Censer

This is an incense burning container that can withstand heat. This is associated with the element of air because it is used to interact with the air via the smoke of the incense.

Centering

Centering is similar to meditation because it is the ability to transfer your consciousness from the physical self to the spiritual self. What that means is that when you center, you can channel your internal energy and escape the external forces that are destroying your energy. The more you practice centering, the easier it will become.

Chakra

Chakra are energy wheels that are found in various sections of your body. The seven primary chakras are root, third-eye, solar plexus, sacral, throat, heart, and crown. You need to find harmony between all these parts to stay mentally, physically, and spiritually balanced. The color red represents your root, which signifies the well-being of your physical body. Your third-eye is indigo, and it is correlated to the middle of your forehead and controls your intuition. Yellow is the color of your solar plexus and is linked to how you feel. Further, your sacral part is orange. Your throat is blue and represents spirituality. Your heart is green and this chakra is linked to astral projection. Finally, your crown is purple, and it is linked to your connection with the cosmos.

Chalice

A chalice is another ritual tool that looks like a goblet. It is commonly associated with the feminine energies. Further, it can be used to drink wine, water, or juice (or anything else really). It is often a consecrated, sacred item that is placed towards the west of your altar. It is used prominently in the Great Rite.

Channeling

Channeling is the act of using psychic powers to speak to a spirit, usually through another host. This term is also used to describe channeling energy, or focusing energy, to complete spells.

Chanting

Chanting is the repetition of certain words during your practice of Wicca. The repetition can be used to bring what you want into fruition. Many incantations will require you to do some chanting. Further, various rituals that you practice with a coven will require this as well. For beginners, chanting can make you feel silly, but once you get the hang of it, it will become an important part of your practice of Wicca.

Charge of the Goddess

The high priestess of a coven normally gives the Charge of the Goddess, which is the words of the Goddess given to her Wiccan "hidden children," who are her followers.

Charge

Charging often refers to crystals, and it is the act of putting energy into an object using magic. It can be done to accomplish several tasks such as luck or protection.

Charms

Charms are objects that have been given magical energy. They are an umbrella term for objects that have been charged, consecrated, or charmed with good energies that will help you accomplish specific tasks. They can be amulets, crystals, or talismans.

Circle

The Wiccan Circle, or more generally a witch's circle, is a sacred space that is created to celebrate, worship the deities, or to create magic. Covens often have certain ways that they will prepare their circles, which can vary greatly, but all circles are sacred spaces. The circle can be created simply by visualization, but it can also be marked with a sacred knife. For Wiccans, the circle is often seen as a transformative place that is between the spirit world and the physical world.

Clairvoyance

Clairvoyance is a psychic skill that allows people to be aware of future events. Not all clairvoyance will have the same level of clarity or the same perceptions of the future. Some clairvoyants won't even be able to tell the future, but instead, they will be able to know about past events that they weren't around for.

Cleansing

To cleanse something means to eliminate any bad energy that it contains. When something is being cleansed, the negativity will be banished from it to ensure nothing nasty lingers. Wiccans often do this daily to make sure that there aren't bad forces near them.

Cone of Power

The cone of power is an abstract concept because the cone can't typically be seen, but it is the power that one or multiple witches create as they are trying to complete a particular task.

Conjuration

Conjuration is using words to evoke a spirit. Many people find this act to be intimidating, but conjuring isn't like what you see in horror movies. If you do it the right way, it doesn't have to be wild and unpredictable. It can be under your control when you channel your energy correctly.

Consecrate

Consecrating something means to cleanse and then bless an object to not just banish the negative energies from it but to add sacred energy to it. Wiccans must be clearer about their purposes when they consecrate an object than when they cleanse it. A clear intention about what they want from the object helps clarify their purposes. Consecrated things have elevated value to Wiccans once they are consecrated.

Corn Doll

A corn doll is a small doll that is usually made to look like a human. Because corn used to refer to all grains in early times, the doll does not have to be made of corn, and it was originally made of agricultural goods to represent fertility. These dolls are still used in various Wiccan rituals, particularly in Europe.

Coven

A person's coven refers to the Wiccans that they worship and do their magic with. Basically, a coven is a witch's church, but covens are generally smaller than your average church. The maximum number of witches in a coven is usually fifteen, but many covens limit themselves to thirteen or less. Covens need at least three people. Not only does a coven do magic together, but they also will celebrate festivals together and are a community that bonds over their shared beliefs.

Covenstead

A covenstead is where witches come together and do their magic. It is their home base, and it is where the coven regularly meets.

Cowan

Cowan is a derogatory term that is used to describe people who are not witches. It is not a term that I would suggest you use because of its derogative nature, but you may hear it in Wiccan groups periodically.

Crone

A crone is one part of the familiar triple goddess archetype, meaning one part of a single deity. The crone is the old woman part of the triple goddess, and she represents wisdom and the end of life.

Crystal Elixir

Crystal elixirs are elixirs that have used crystals. To create these elixirs, you place crystals in water and other liquids, often with other herbs and items thrown in. The energy that the crystal adds to the elixir can be beneficial in witchcraft. These elixirs are often drunk and used for healing or improved magic.

Cross-Quarter Days

This term is what the Fire festivals, Samhain, Imbolc, Beltane, and Lamma, are called. They are four of the eight major festivals in the Wiccan religion.

Crystal Ball

A glass or crystal ball that you can use for scrying.

Curses

These are spells that put malevolence upon other people.

Dawning Down the Sun

Dawning down the sun means to invoke God into oneself. Witches can increase their powers through this ritual.

Days of Power

Days of power are the times when witches are at their most powerful. These days include your birthday, Blood of the Moon, anniversaries of being initiated, Sabbats, and miscellaneous astrological happenings.

Dedication

Dedication is a process that witches go through when they accept the Wiccan path and strive to reach an adept status someday. This process occurs before initiation, and it lasts for a year plus one day commonly, but the exact process may differ depending on your coven.

Degrees of Witchcraft

In witchcraft, witches will have different levels of skill, which are called degrees. The degrees that you must go through will depend on the coven, but generally, they are as follows: neophyte, middle stage, and full membership. The clergy is also held at a different level, a fourth-degree, in many Wiccan covens.

Deflection

This process generally uses a mirror to deflect evil forces away from you. When you deflect, you take bad energy and put it onto something else.

Deity

Deities refer to gods and goddesses who have supreme power. These beings are not human and have unique powers and properties. Wiccans celebrate multiple deities and often focus on the God and the Goddess as the two most prominent forces.

Deosil

Deosil means that, in a ritual, motions must be made in a clockwise manner. Many rituals will require you to act in this manner. It is commonly used in the northern hemisphere and represents good energies.

Divination

Divination is the process of obtaining knowledge about the future, present, or past. It often uses psychic abilities like clairvoyance, crystal balls, tarot cards, or scrying. It refers to all the methods you could use to get some knowledge that ordinary people would never have. While divination often uses tools, it doesn't have to. You can divine using simple things you have around the house.

Dowsing

Dowsing is the practice of using a pendulum, forks, or rods in magic to find a location. These tools can be used with a variety of methods.

Drawing Down the Moon

This practice means to invoke the Goddess into oneself. It is a way of channeling the divine and becoming more powerful.

Earth Power

Earth power refers to the energies that you can find in earthly objects like pants, rocks, and crystals. Wiccans believe that all these things have energies. Thus, they can be used for magical purposes.

Eke Name

This is a name that you have that is only used in divine spaces. It is secret to anyone but your fellow worshippers or the deities.

Elder

Elder is a title usually given to third-degree witches who are older than the others and commonly are known for being wise. Only some Wiccan groups have this distinction.

Elements

The five elements are part of many rituals. Some witches specialize in using certain elements, and they feel more akin to certain elements than others. The elements are fire, water, air, earth, and spirit, which make up the earth and everything that is on it. These elements can be used to increase the power of your spells because they tap into nature and allow you to focus on your intentions more easily.

Equinox

Equinoxes happen twice a year, and they are the time when the sun goes over the equator. They mark certain Wiccan holidays.

Esbat

Esbat is when witches gather, usually around the time of the full moon.

Familiars

Familiars are animals or other non-human spirits that guide witches. They allow witches to magnify their powers and better focus their energy. These familiars can be your pets or any creature that you feel helps you better your magic and focus your powers.

Five-Fold Kiss

The five-fold kiss is done before entering a ritual circle, and witches will kiss five spots: feet, knees, stomach, breasts, and lips. You do not have to do this ritual if you do not feel comfortable with it.

Fluffy Bunny

This idea is a term used to mock practitioners who are seen as being shallow in their practice of Wicca.

Great Rite

The Great Rite is a sexual ritual that uses sex to create more energy and focus the power of two witches. It is especially essential on the festival of Beltane as well as other special occasions.

Grimoire

A grimoire is a term that refers to written down spells or accounts of witchcraft. A Book of Shadows is a type of grimoire, but any book with magical properties in it can be a grimoire.

Group Practitioner

A group practitioner is a witch who does magic within a coven rather than alone. Wiccans are encouraged to be group practitioners and to join covens to celebrate their religious beliefs and practice white magic. For some people, the group element of Wicca is important.

Handfasting

Handfasting is the Wicca version of a marriage ceremony.

High Priest or Priestess

The high priest and priestesses are the leaders of their covens.

Hiving Off

Hiving off is when people leave one coven to start a new one and branch off from their original group. Hiving off allows the Wiccan religion to grow and expand without covens becoming too big.

Incantation

An incantation is a spell that uses words to craft your intentions and bring them to life. You've probably heard of incantations before, such as abracadabra. They can be as simple or as complex as you want them to be.

Initiation

Initiation is allowing new members to become part of a coven. During initiation, the person joining the coven will acknowledge that they want to join the group and reaffirm that they believe in what their new coven believes in. Several rituals take place during the initiation.

Intentions

Intentions are some of the most important parts of magic. Whenever you do magic, it is crucial to have an intention behind it, which is a clear idea of what you want to happen when you cast your spell.

Invoke

When you invoke in a ritual, you call upon the deities to give you energy and support.

Lady and Lord

Lady and Lord are ways that people sometimes refer to the God and the Goddess. These terms can also be used to show reverence for the High Priest or Priestess.

Left-Hand Path

The left-hand path refers to using black magic, and it is not a path that Wiccans are permitted to go on.

Libation

Libation is an offering of wine or water that you pour on the altar after you complete a ritual. You do this to show respect and gratitude to the God and the Goddess.

Lunar Eclipse

This occasion is a special occasion that celebrates the Goddess' aspects such as the crone.

Magical Alphabets

Some Wiccan traditions use magical alphabets in their rituals, spells, and books of shadows. Magical alphabets are basically just codes to keep your information secret. The need to keep this info secret isn't as great as it once was, but some Wiccans still use magical alphabets such as the Theban alphabet, which is a common magical alphabet.

Magick

Magick is a term often used by witches to separate witchcraft from stage magic. Aleister Crowley, sometimes known as Uncle A, was likely the one to add the K to magic. Many witches, including Wiccans, add the K when they do magic.

Maiden

Maiden, or maid, is the first part of the triple goddess, meaning that she is one part of the overall goddess. She represents youth.

Manifest

Manifestation is being able to channel your mental energy to make what you wish to come true a reality. Manifestation uses several methods, such as visualization, intentions, and even lucid dreams, which are dreams that you can consciously control.

Merry Meet

This is a phrase used to greet other Wiccans.

Mother

Mother is one of the parts of the triple goddess. She is the middle-aged part that represents fertility and motherhood.

Necromancy

Necromancy means dealing with dead people in your magic. Witches often try to deal with spirits and communicate with them for information. Necromancy is often scary for the new witch, but it doesn't have to be dark, and it can be incredibly rewarding.

Neophyte

A neophyte is someone who has just joined a coven and has not yet been initiated. Neophytes will have to take time to learn the craft before joining as a full member of the coven. A neophyte is called a wiclet in specific settings.

Numerology

Numerology is a method of divination that uses numbers and formulas to find answers. Each number corresponds to a letter from the alphabet, and this process is often used when you want to get a witch name or a name within your coven. Numerology is especially appealing to people who love to work with numbers, but even if you aren't a numbers person, it is manageable.

Occult

Occult is a word that means the study of the "covert secrets of the universe." It often explores supernatural elements of the world, but it also studies witchcraft and witches. The occult has long been misunderstood and is often viewed as scary, but it is not as terrifying as it may seem in horror films.

Omen

An omen is a sign that suggests that something might happen. It can either be a good omen or a bad one.

Pagan

Pagan refers to all religions that aren't Abrahamic. It includes Wicca, but it also includes many more religions that aren't necessarily associated with witchcraft.

Palm Reading

One form of divination is palm reading. Palm reading uses the lines and ridges of your hands to predict your future. It takes time to learn all the meanings for palm reading, but it is a rewarding craft.

Pantheistic

Wiccans are pantheistic, meaning that they see divine energy everywhere they go. Everything in life has that divine energy, and even non-living things are considered to be part of the divine.

Pantheon

A pantheon is a selection of deities that a particular religion accepts. Some religions have rigidly decided gods, but in some Wiccan groups, Wiccans are allowed to choose from the pantheon of the deities.

Pendulum

Pendulums are objects that are attached to ropes of chains, and they are then moved back and forth, and you can use them for dowsing.

Pentacle

The pentacle is one of the most important symbols in the Wiccan religion. It is a star with five points, and it represents the five elements— earth, air, fire, water, and spirit. Witches, including Wiccans, often have talismans and charms that have the pentacle on it, and they also use it for their rituals.

Pentagram

A pentagram, like a pentacle, is a star with five points, but in its history, it has taken on connotations that don't represent what Wicca stands for, which is why a pentacle is more commonly considered the primary Wiccan symbol. Pentagrams have become associated with Satanism, which makes pentagrams seem like something they are not.

Personal Power

Your personal power is the power that keeps your body running and allows it to do magic. It was given to you by the Goddess and the God through their own power. Everyone has their own kinds of powers and special abilities that other people don't have.

Planes

These are the various levels of existence. Some examples of the planes are: Physical, spiritual, etheric, astral, and mental. You can become more aware of these planes via magic.

Potion

A potion is a liquidy mix made with herbs and other magical ingredients. It is made to be part of various rituals.

Prana

All living things are part of the cosmic order, and that is prana, the energy of all that are culminating in a strong force.

Precognition

Precognition is the psychic ability to know what the future holds. Some people have a stronger sense of the future than others.

Projective Energy

Projective energy is the energy that sends things away from you. You can use this energy to get rid of negative forces by channeling positive ones. Your dominant hand is your projective hand. Thus, right-handed people use their right hands for projective energy while left-handed people use their left-hands for projective energy.

Receptive Energy

Receptive energy is pulling forces towards you. Many people use crystals to bring in good energy. Your non-dominant hand is your receptive hand, so if you are right-handed, your left hand is your receptive hand. If you are left-handed, your right hand is your receptive hand.

Reincarnation

Reincarnation is the belief that a person goes through multiple physical bodies. They are reborn to learn and become better souls. Each time people are reborn, they take on a new form based on what they need to advance and improve as beings; thus, people may go through multiple bodies, not even all of them human, throughout life.

Right-Hand Path

This path is the path of goodness, the Wiccan Rede, and white magic. It is using your magic for good rather than selfish and evil purposes that result in harming others.

Ritual

A ritual refers to any action that channels and concentrates your energy to accomplish one predetermined task. Rituals are repeated behaviors that follow the same patterns, and you can have rituals within religious contexts as well outside of religion.

Rule of Three

The rule of three is an important Wiccan belief. While not all Wiccans believe it, many do. The idea is that the energy that a Wiccan puts out into the world be returned in threes, so it is basically the Wiccan version of karma. If you do bad, that bad will be returned to you three times over. If you do good, that good will also be returned to you three times over.

Runes

Runes are symbols that witches commonly carve into objects. They are widely found on candles and wood.

Sabbats

The sabbats are the eight festivals that are celebrated by Wiccans. These festivals mark the seasonal changes that occur each year, and the equinoxes and the solstices mark them. On these sabbats, witches have increased power, and they have certain rituals that they will complete based on their coven. These rituals may include things like a balefire or a yule log.

Scourge

A scourge is a whip that is used by Wiccans in rituals. While this sounds harsh, often, the scourges are made of soft materials like silk because the scourge is more symbolic than anything else.

Scrying

Another method of divination is scrying. Scrying is using objects like water or a crystal ball to create visions of the future.

Séance

When you have a séance, you speak with the spirits. These spirits can either be dead people or other entities.

Shadow Work

In the Wiccan world, shadows represent the dark side of people. This does not mean that shadow work is dark magic. Rather, shadow work entails using the dark part of yourself to do good work. Shadow work can create a balance for people who have been traumatized or hurt. Shadow work is healing for witches with hurt bodies and souls because it allows them to construct something out of the darkness.

Sigils

Sigils are similar to runes because they are symbols that are used in Wiccan magic. They are drawings or other illustrations that Wiccans carry along with them to illustrate their intentions before casting a spell or brewing a potion.

Skyclad

Skyclad refers to when witches do rituals in the nude. Not all types of Wiccans do naked work, but Alexandrian Wiccans or Gardernarian Wiccans are known for working alone and doing so naked. Being naked while casting spells is not something that everyone would enjoy, but for those who do it, it is liberating, and it allows them to do magic with fewer limits.

Smudging

Smudging is the practice of using smoke or incense to cleanse places or items. It is often done with herbs as well.

Solstice

Each year, there are two solstices, and these solstices mark the shortest and longest days of the year. Solstices are vital because they align with the festivals that Wiccans celebrate.

Solar Eclipse

A solar eclipse is a special occasion for Wiccans, and it celebrates aspects of the God, such as Death and Dark Lord.

Solitary Practitioner

A solitary practitioner is a witch who works alone and is not part of a coven. Wicca is often done in covens because of how communal it is, but some people practice the teaching of Wicca without being in a formal coven. This practice may be the only option for people who are in rural places where covens aren't familiar. Some people prefer to work alone even when they have opportunities to be in covens, and that is perfectly okay.

Spell

A spell is a type of magic that uses a specific goal to drive the magic. You can accomplish a spell in millions of ways, and they often include elements such as candles, incantations, and sigils. Spells may also be done at an altar, especially when they are part of religious rituals. You can easily customize spells and make them your own.

Spirits of the Stones

The spirits of the stones means that there are energies tied to the elements of Earth, fire, air, and water that are linked to each of the four directions within the Wiccan circle.

Spiritualism

Spiritualism is believing that the dead can communicate with people who are still alive by going through mediums.

Summerlands

The Summerlands is an afterworld that is like heaven. It is often associated with reincarnation and as a break and time for rest between physical lives.

Summoner

The summoner is a male clergy member who assists the High Priest in the coven. He transmits information to the Maiden.

Talisman

A talisman is an object, usually one that is small, that witches can bring with them to places for good luck and keep bad energy away. A talisman can be pretty much anything. Even something as small as a charm or a slip of paper can be a good talisman.

Tarot Cards

Tarot cards are a method of divination. In this practice, you use a deck of 78 cards, and you turn them over to figure out what the future will hold. Tarot is a fun, easy, and inexpensive form of divination that you can start practicing right away!

The Craft

The craft is another name for witchcraft.

Transmutation

Transmutation means that one thing turns into another form. Natural objects often experience transmutation, and this property can be used in spells to do things such as turning negative energy into positive energy.

Triple Goddess

A triple goddess is one goddess that is made up of three entities. Usually, she is made up of the crone, the maiden, and the mother, who are each representative of a life stage that women go through—youth, motherhood, and old age. All these beings come together to make one single goddess.

Undine

An undine is a creature that lives in the water. Witches include nymphs and mermaids in this category.

Vision Quest

Vision questing is the process of either using astral projection or dreams to complete a specific goal. This action is also commonly known as pathworking, and it can be a highly rewarding activity for witches.

Wand

A wand is a small, thin stick usually made of wood that can hold power so that witches can focus their energy on a particular thing. The wand helps them ensure that they keep their focus on where they need it to be. Wands are not necessary, but they are fun.

Warding

Warding is a protection tactic that witches use to block off their home from negative forces. Wards are spiritual barriers that keep everyone in the home safe, which is why witches so often put them up. When you make a ward, you are keeping your vital spaces safe. Wards are particular areas that you do not want negative energies to influence.

Warlock

Warlock is a word that witches sometimes use to describe people who use magic for evil. It is not the male version of a witch. Witch is a gender-neutral term, and it applies to all Wiccans and practitioners of witchcraft. A male Wiccan would not feel comfortable if you called him a warlock because of the negative views linked to being a warlock.

Wheel of the Year

The wheel of the year is the Wiccan calendar. It is a cyclical calendar that is broken down by the eight festivals that Wiccans celebrate. The whole wheel is the entire year, completed by the eight Sabbats. The Wiccans focus on the cycle of life rather than a linear view of time. This calendar was created based on the Celtic calendar that people created before the Gregorian calendar existed.

White Magic

White magic is the opposite of black magic. When you use white magic, you choose only to use your magic for benevolent causes. You do not try to harm anyone with your powers. Wiccans use white magic and they prohibit black magic.

Wiccan Rede

The Wiccan Rede is a relevant Wiccan code that urges practitioners not to harm anyone with their magic. Wiccans are discouraged from doing any black magic, and while they are encouraged to do magic, harmful magic is inherently anti-Wicca.

Wiccaning

A wiccaning is a way of welcoming an infant into the Wiccan community. It is similar to the Christian concept of baptism. A Wiccaning is an essential rite of passage for a Wiccan family with a newborn, and during this rite, the child is given energies that will keep them safe and happy. This concept is one of the most exciting rituals in the Wiccan faith because it is a way of ushering in new life into the Wiccan covens. Children will not have to continue the Wiccan religion, but they are introduced to the community during their Wiccans. It is up to the parents whether they want to have a wiccaning at all.

Widdershins

Widdershins refers to the counter-clockwise direction. This term is used by witches in some rituals and spells, especially in the southern hemisphere. Even in the southern hemisphere, this is sometimes being replaced with clockwise motions.

Witch

To put it briefly, a witch is someone who practices witchcraft. Most Wiccans consider themselves witches (but some branches don't like the term witch), but not all witches are Wiccans. Wicca is a religion so that anyone can choose witchcraft, but not everyone will want to follow Wicca.

Witchcraft

Surely, by now, you know what witchcraft is, but it is the practice and crafting of magic.

Witches Ladder

This term is a string that has four beads in it or four knots that are sometimes used by Wiccans.

Witching Hour

This term refers to midnight.

Zodiac

The zodiac is an astrological concept that uses your birth to assign signs. The zodiac is rooted in twelve constellations and uses these constellations. Astrologers use the celestial bodies to make predictions about what people are like and what will happen to them. For many Wiccans, divine activity and astrology can be used to help with their witchcraft practices.

CHAPTER 3
Wiccan Rites and Celebrations

The Wheel of the Year

The wheel of the year refers to the Wiccan calendar that dictates when the Sabbats or the sun celebrations take place. There are also moon celebrations that occur each month during the full moon called esbats. These eight festivals are rooted in the Celtic festivals that were oriented around agriculture. Wiccans have shifted the festivals slightly and have reinvented them in ways that maintain some of the Celtic ideals but also take on a life of their own. These festivals are often times for Wiccans to practice certain rituals, but they are also times in which Wiccans are most potent.

Samhain

Samhain is a holiday that you probably already know— Halloween. It takes place on October 31st, and it marks the summer ending and the days becoming shorter. The Celts began this celebration on what is now known as All Hallows Eve, which carried into November 1st and became the Christian's All Saints' Day. Samhain is a holiday that marks people best being able to communicate with the spirits because Wiccans believe that the veil between our world and the spirit world is thinner on Samhain. For Wiccans, Samhain is the beginning of the calendar, and it represents celebrating the last of summer's bounty to enter a more scary winter.

Yule

The festival of Yule marks the winter solstice, which is the day when the night is longest. This festival occurs near December 21st, but it is slightly different each year. Another Christian holiday closely aligns with this one— Christmas— showing how pre-Christian religions influence many of the Christian festivals. Yule is one of the quieter festivals, and there are less gatherings around this time. Wiccans will give fights around this time and light candles on Midwinter Eve. They even use pine decorations and holly! If you've ever heard of a yule log, it is through pagan tradition that the idea came to be. In old times, pagans would burn a log to represent the holiday.

Imbolc

Imbolc is the third Wiccan holiday that takes place on February 1. It marks the beginning of spring, even though February doesn't feel like spring in most of the world. Again, it corresponds with the Christian feast day of St. Brigid, who legend says was based on the Celtic goddess Brigid. Imbolc is all about things reawakening and life starting to flourish again after the long winter. Many new members of individual covens are brought in around this time, and a lot of the rituals include lighting candles. It is a time to get back to focusing on the Wiccan religion and reorient your perspective.

Ostara

Ostara is a holiday that takes place around March 21, and it aligns with the spring equinox. The Christians have Easter, but Wiccans have Ostara. Ostara is a festival that marks fertility because, during this time, you can start to see spring come into bloom. In ancient times, this fertility was often represented by bunnies and eggs, which you see carry on into modern times. During this holiday, the Goddess is said to be in her maiden form. She and the young God are getting closer to conceiving their child who is said to be born on Yule. Ostara is a time for Wiccans to realign themselves with what they want to accomplish and send life through those goals. It is about reviving and reenergizing things that winter had left stagnant and slow.

Beltane

Beltane is the last of the three fertility festivals that usher in spring, and it occurs on May 1st. The veil between the spirit and mortal world is again thinner on Beltane because Beltane is the polar opposite of Samhain on the calendar. For Wiccans, this festival is often highly sexual because it was when the Maiden Goddess and the God went through the great rite (marriage), and their union marked the culmination of the growing fertility from the months prior. Beltane often is a fun festival that includes things like bonfires and sleeping under the stars. It is a typical time for handfasting and finding love.

Litha

Litha, also Midsummer, marks the summer solstice, which is usually around June 21st. The God is most powerful on this day because it marks the day when the days stop growing longer and begin to dwindle. Litha is a festival that celebrates the brightness of summer and often includes bonfires to hold onto the summer light for as long as possible. Further, it marks the coming harvest. Wiccans commonly do rituals outside during Litha, and they are filled with joy. Also, they make the most of the spells that use the sun. It is no doubt the brightest of Wiccan holidays.

Lammas

Lammas occurs on August 1, and it represents the beginning of harvest. Grain would be collected during this time, and people would be able to bake bread after not having fresh grain all winter. In some traditions, it is called Lughnasadh from the Celtic god, Lugh. During this time the Sun God becomes weaker, and he starts to make his descent towards death before being revived when Yule comes around. Lammas is a time when Wiccans are thankful. It is a great time for an appreciation ceremony. It was an important time for ancient people, and it continues to be important to pagans today.

Mabon

Mabon is the final festival on the Wiccan calendar, and it occurs around September 21, during the autumnal equinox. This festival marks the time when winter is coming near, but it is still a time of harvest when nuts and fruits are ready to be collected. During this time, Wiccans often look back at the year and celebrate what their work has brought them. It is a time of great abundance, which means that it is a good time for spells that are related to prosperity. It is also a good time for being gracious. Mabon is often bittersweet because it marks the decline towards winter. Many Wiccans bake a lot during this time and have foods made from the goods of harvest. They also use cornucopias as centerpieces. They indulge in cider and pies, and they preserve fruits and vegetables throughout the year. This festival also marks the cycle of old age for the deities. Wiccans may spend this time appreciating the outdoors while they still can or giving offerings to their altar. It is one of the last holidays that they can do extensive outdoor activities. Cities also have ceremonies and festivities to celebrate Pagan Pride Day during Mabon.

Wiccan Rites

Like any religion, Wicca has rites of passage that Wiccans celebrate. During these times, they go through certain rituals that the elders of the community will guide, and everyone will take part in it. These rituals are outside of the holidays, but they take place near the festivals and are used as part of the festival celebrations as well. These rites are important to Wiccans, and they allow Covens to change and grow. Further, they enable witchcraft to spread and to flourish. Without rites, Wicca would be lacking many of the religious qualities that makes it appeal to so many people who are looking for direction

Dedication

The dedication ceremony is a ceremony that marks a Wiccan deciding to become dedicated to the Wiccan religion and the deities. This ceremony can happen when there is a new moon, but it can also occur whenever the person chooses and feels that they want to be dedicated to the Wiccan faith. This ceremony will require incense, sacred oil, and candles. It is done around the altar. The dedication marks a member's beginning with the Wiccan faith, and it allows them to become part of a community that is bigger than themselves.

Wiccaning

Wiccanings are a way of welcoming a newborn into the Wiccan community. Sometimes, it is called a "baby-naming ceremony" or a sainting. This practice is similar to the Christian celebration of baptism. Although, when a child goes through a Wiccaning, they do not have to belong to the Wiccan faith. Wicca emphasizes that each person in Wicca must determine themselves that they want to be part of it. Thus, the child may choose to join Wicca, but they are not committed to it. A high priest or priestess commits this rite, but it can also be done by the parents of the child sometimes. This ceremony also gives other members of the coven a chance to bless the child and celebrate that child.

Handfasting

Handfasting is the Wiccan equivalent to a marriage ceremony. It represents two people being linked together. People who choose to partake in this do not need to have the intention of getting legally married, but they also may use it as an opportunity to wed as well legally. This ceremony is generally completed by members of the clergy, often a high priest or priestess. It is rooted in Celtic traditions that called for people's arms to be tied together with ribbon to represent being unified forever, which is why today we call marriage "tying the knot." This rite can be custom fit to what you want it to be to match your expectations for your handfasting.

Handparting

Handparting is the opposite of handfasting. It is a ceremony that Wiccans use to divorce people when they were unified in a handfasting ceremony. It also does not count as a legal divorce. Usually, a Wiccan leader will complete this ceremony. It is done using the ribbon that was used for the couple's handfasting ceremony. The relationship is then severed. It is a somewhat sad ceremony, but it allows couples to part and move on with their lives without having an unwanted connection, so while it is bittersweet, it is sometimes needed.

Appreciation

An appreciation rite is a rite that Wiccans use when they want to show respect to the natural world as well as the divine and spirit worlds. This ritual is all about gratitude, and it is a way that Wiccans reassert everything that they believe in. Wiccans can choose what they want to be grateful for based on their type of Wicca and what their coven decides. There are no firm rules. This rite is often practiced on sabbats, especially during harvest, but it is appropriate at any time.

Funeral

In the Wiccan religion, a funeral is commonly called a Summerland service. This rite marks the end of a person's life. A Wiccan funeral is similar to most other funerals in that it allows people to celebrate the life of the dead and to remember stories about that person. This ceremony allows healing to begin and can include several qualities such as poetry, eulogies, and prayers.

CHAPTER 4
Mesmerizing Magic

Types of Witches

Within the Wiccan witch distinction, there are several other types of witches that you can be based on the types of witchcraft that you can do. You don't have to identify as one of these types, but these types can help you understand what you like to do most in witchcraft and find other people who have similar interests. These types of witches mainly help you see the variety of spells and attitudes that witches can have. They can all use crystals as part of their craft, but they have different areas of emphasis when they use those crystals.

Cottage Witches

A cottage witch is a witch who is energized by pursuits related to the home. They often do most of their spells in the home, and they enjoy making their homesteads and the people in them happy. People who enjoy domestic activities are likely to be cottage witches, also known as hearth witches. These witches will want to make sure their homes are extra protected, and they will tend to use tools like brooms or other homestead items in their spells. While cottage witches are not limited by religion, they can be Wiccan if they choose.

Crystal Witches

There is a special distinction of witches who tend to use crystals primarily in their work. Any other witch category can include the use of crystals, but crystal witches use crystals in most or all of their spells. If you are interested in crystals, you don't have to identify as a crystal witch, but if you find yourself drawn to crystals and want to work with them constantly, this may be a perfect distinction for you. Crystal witches will use several methods that include crystals such as crystal therapy or crystal in meditation. A crystal witch would feel incomplete without their crystals.

Eclectic Witches

Eclectic witches are witches who combine different parts of witchcraft and have no main area of focus. They like to try a myriad of methods, and they go by whatever feels right for them at the time. Most witches probably fall into this category. Wiccans who don't fall into other categories often just call themselves Wiccan rather than eclectic.

Green Witches

Green witches are witches that have a special connection with nature. They love to keep plants around and often have fresh herbs that they use in their spells. Green witches often will use a combination of herbs and crystals when they are doing crystal magic, but they may also channel other natural elements. Green witches love the great outdoors, so they may practice their witchcraft outside and away from their houses to feel more connected to greenery.

Hedge Witches

Hedge witches are witches who combine the elements of cottage witches and green witches. They like natural features, including crystals, but they also want to focus on their homesteads and their relationships to spirits. These witches were seen initially as wise old women, and they got their name from living just beyond villages (they were on the hedge between the village and the natural world). They combine the appeals of nature and the home, and they like to incorporate magic in every part of their lives. Often, they do want to work alone, but some hedge witches do join covens and are part of religions like Wicca.

Kitchen Witches

Kitchen witches are similar to cottage witches, but they focus on the domestic duties of the kitchen. They often love to use spells that relate to cooking and use cauldrons frequently. They spend much of their time in their kitchens, and they can use crystals to improve the quality of their meals and other concoctions. Some kitchen witches will keep their altar in their kitchen, and they will probably cast most of their spells there, even the non-kitchen related ones. These witches make great dinner party hosts! Like green witches, they may like to mix herbs or other edible elements with their crystals to prepare for more powerful spells.

Spirit Working Witches

Spirit working witches are witches who often participate in necromancy and other elements of the spirit world. They strive to communicate with spirits and use psychic abilities to connect with the dead. They often use crystal magic in their practice both for spells, maintaining good energies, and scrying.

Tasks to Get Started

Readying Your Altar

You will need to start preparing your altar by determining what space you want to have your altar in. It can be any space that you choose. You can use a full room to hold your altar, or you can use just a tiny portion of that room. It doesn't matter what you choose to be the space as your altar. As long as your area fits your needs, it is perfect. You don't need to make a massive investment of your space or get a new house to have a sufficient altar. Work with what you have and go from there.

What you need for the altar itself is a space that is a flat space. You can use things such as a table, a box, or a desk, among other things. Try to ensure that your space isn't made of a material that would conduct electricity for safety reasons because your tools may be conducive. Again, you don't have to have the world's prettiest altar. If you have the resources to make it look nicer, that is great, but the point of the altar is for worship. It doesn't have to win any prizes. Make your altar something that fits your tastes because you have to live with it.

You'll want to try to set up your altar in a room that you have cleansed with sea salt or another cleansing agent of your choice. You'll also want to cast a purification spell on the room. If you can set up your altar outdoors, you will not have to cleanse or purify your space because it is part of nature. You'll want to set up the altar in the middle of the room and ensure that when you look at the altar, you are looking towards the east.

In the space around the altar, you should draw a circle, which is an important circle in the Wiccan rituals. You can make this circle using various things like chalk, but it can also be drawn only in your imagination. Do whatever makes you feel most comfortable in your worship or follow whatever your type of Wiccanism suggests.

You'll need various tools and adornments for your altar based on the type of Wicca you practice. The Gardnerians, for example, need eight tools while the Saxons only need a knife, a spear, and a sword. You could even choose to branch out from all other denominations and make up your own rules and choose whatever equipment you want to use when you practice Wicca. You will want to make sure that your tools are cleansed before you use and you'll also want to charge them with energy.

Most witches across Wiccan denominations will require a special knife, called an athame, in their craft. It is sometimes referred to by different names in various types of Wicca, but the knife should be something that you like and fits you individually. You can choose how big the knife is and what style of handle you want. You can buy the knife online or in stores. It doesn't have to be a special knife beyond the special attributes that you give it through your magic. If you can, you'll want to have your Wiccan name etched into the blade of the knife. Or, if you can't have it engraved, you can put your name on any part of it by writing your name in marker or using a label. Some other tools that you may need for use at your altar are a wand, a bell, a sword, and a pentacle. Again, this will vary depending on your practice. You may also be required to wear a robe or practice skyclad.

You'll want to have certain adornments for your altar to ensure that it is ready for use. Many witches like to have candles and incense on their altars because Wiccans often use both incense and candles in their practices. White candles are always good options because they are the most versatile, but different candles will have different meanings, as will various incenses.

You will also want a few dishes to hold things like salt and water as well as a libation dish, which is a dish that is used when Wiccans first pour their ritual wine/fruit juice for a ritual to the gods.

Relatedly, you'll also want goblets for the same ritual. The high priest or priestess will have their goblets on the altar.

Additionally, you can place representations of the deities onto your altar. They can be whatever objects you want that remind you of the deities. They can be using photos, statues, or representative objects. Feel free to be creative with these items.

Wiccans traditionally follow specific rules for their altars, so follow those as best as you are able based on your type of Wiccanism. You should also know that as long as you are worshipping candidly, your efforts are valid even if they don't follow the letter of the law. Wiccanism, especially as a broad concept, is open to possibility and is flexible. However, some traditional practices of it will be more rigid.

Keep an Open Mind

When you begin witchcraft, you will need to keep an open mind. Many people close themselves off to the possibility of witchcraft before they have even considered it properly. Your magic will be limited. It isn't like what you see in movies about witches. It is much more subtle, but it is still well worth the effort that you will put into it. Don't close your mind off because you feel silly or assume witchcraft isn't for you. Witchcraft and Wicca are for everyone who wants to take part.

CHAPTER 5
Crystal Magic

Crystals are some of the most magnificent tools that you can use in Wiccan witchcraft. They contain so much power and possibility. It can take some time to get used to using crystals and to figure out how to best use them to your advantage, but it is well worth the effort that you will put in. Crystals will help keep you safe, allow you to manifest your dreams, and help you combat normal life problems that may stand in your way of happiness. These crystals, radiant stones, come in a variety of forms, and each form can be used for various purposes. Much of crystal magic is personalized based on a witch's experiences, but there are some common associations and basic rules that most Wiccans follow when it comes to crystal magic.

History of Crystal Magic

People have been using crystals to create magic for thousands of years, and they have done so without having to stop and think about it. It came naturally. Before crystals themselves were recognized, stone was acknowledged, which is a broader group that crystals fall under. These stones were seen as a way to build early societies, and some of the first buildings were religious in nature, showing how stones were immediately used as a way of worship. The stones connected the natural world to realms far beyond the Earth's plane. People were already learning that through the parts of the Earth, they could connect to things far beyond themselves. Stones were transformative in ways that excited humans.

The magic of stone was first recognized (or at least the first that we know of) 11,000 years ago when a temple was built from stone in Turkey. Further, humans continued to recognize the amazing properties of the stones that were part of our Earth as they continued to build sacred places from stone and eventually began to build houses from the stone. Stone remains an integral part of our lives. It builds the world around us, and it is a tool we have taken from earth to protect ourselves. It represents our alignment with our Earth and our ability to harness parts of the Earth to use the Earth's energies to our advantage.

Stones started to grow far beyond parts for shelter. They became sacred. People began carrying stones with them for luck, and they began to see that there was more to stone than they realized. Soon, they would start seeing the beautiful wonder of crystals, which help so much more power than early humans would have ever guessed. The early wishing stones that humans carried were not quite as beautiful as the crystals we know today, but they were still precious, and they would bring good fortune upon the people who carried them.

Remember that Wiccans believe that non-living things still have energies, which includes stones. Among the stones are some of the most precious stones that exist, which are crystals. Crystals are stones that are generally found in huge mounds of rock, and they were made from minerals below the Earth's surface. After years of formulating, crystals formed and became stones filled with color, looking more magical than ever. Early people recognized with wonderment what the pretty stones could do right away. Aboriginal people embraced crystals, as did people in ancient Greece, Rome, and Egypt. They would carry the crystals around as talismans, and the gems became an essential part of their rituals, including death rituals.

Crystals continue to be relevant to people who have found new ways to tap into the power of crystals. We have discovered the healing properties of crystals and the ability to balance ourselves with them. Through magic, we can realign our energies and reduce all the negativity in our lives. Crystals don't just help one part of our lives, but they tap into each component and allow us to engage with ourselves and others in unique ways. Wiccans use crystals in special ways. Some people limit their crystal use to only healing, but Wiccans use them in most parts of their practice. They use them for rituals and spells. They incorporate them into as many areas of their lives as possible and they use those crystals to get in touch with the divine. There's no limit to what a Wiccan can do with crystals. Crystals are a magnificent part of Earth, so they can be used to better our connection to all parts of existence, and we can learn through crystals how to help ourselves and others thrive merely by embracing the energies around us.

Commonly Used Crystals

If you want to use crystals properly, it helps to know which crystals are some of the most prominent and powerful ones that Wiccans and other witches commonly use. Further, it helps to understand the general symbolism and powers that the gems contain because by knowing this, you will be able to craft your spells beyond the ones provided in this book. While it does help to be given some starting spells, part of the joy of witchcraft is learning to craft your own magic given the tools around you. While there are organized aspects of Wicca, there are still many personal liberties that allow you to be creative with your witchcraft. You can use crystals in conjunction with other magical elements such as candles, spells, or sigils, but crystals are also pretty compelling on their own, so it's up to you to decide how they best work for you! There's no right or wrong way to practice magic (beyond the Wiccan Rede), so it will take some experimentation before you know what you like best.

Amber

Amber is actually not a crystal, but although it is the sap from a tree, it can be used as a crystal in witchcraft because of its crystal-like properties. This crystal's chakra is the solar plexus, so it is especially helpful in spells that help you with willpower or tasks associated with your personality because the solar plexus is the central part of your personality. Amber can also be beneficial in improving your self-confidence. Amber is an easy crystal to find, and it can both amplify and absorb energy. It works well on its own, but it also pairs well with clear quartz (aka quartz crystal). Its honey-colored appearance makes it quite recognizable.

Amethyst

Amethyst is one of the most popular and pretty of all the magical crystals (and other stones that are grouped in with crystals). This stone is the gemstone of Aquarians, who might find it extra powerful. It is a purple color, and this color can range from being a light to a deep purple. It is ruled by the third-eye of the chakra and the crown chakra, meaning that it is associated with both insight into the internal and external worlds, but it also helps us stay aligned with nature and grounded to the Earth. It also provides internal peace.

Amethyst is a stone that's known for accomplishing many things beyond what. It is known to help people with addictions or who struggle to balance healthy and indulgent parts of themselves because it was often known to ancient Greeks as a "sober stone," because it was said to help ameliorate the negative effects of alcohol. Further, this stone's high vibration means that it is great at converting negative energy into positive energy. It also helps magnify intelligence, intuition, and psychic skills. Thus, amethyst is one of the most transformative stones there is. It helps spiritually guide people and heals them. It is one of the most versatile crystals, which means you'll probably want to have it around.

To sum up the key pluses of amethyst, some of the main ways that this crystal can help you with are sleep issues, being more creative, balancing your worry, and helping you with addiction. This crystal also works well with clear quartz and citrine. The more you practice using amethyst, the better you will become at tapping into all of its power. Not only does it look pretty, but it can transform your life.

Ametrine

Ametrine is a special crystal that is the combination of citrine and amethyst. Thus, this crystal will have both the yellow and the purple parts of it that represent each gem that it contains. Further, ametrine allows you to combine the properties of citrine and amethyst and magnify their impacts for amazing results. As a combination crystal, you can get more bang for your buck, and moreover, this gem is gorgeous, so it would be nice to look at even if its magical qualities weren't so great.

Ametrine is associated with all the chakra that citrine and amethyst are, so it rules over the solar plexus, the third-eye, and the crown. Thus, it is linked to having plenty, lessening negativity, creating balance among energies, handling personality, and enabling psychic powers. Citrine can be used in conjunction with citrine, amethyst, and clear quartz to tap into its power even more!

Apatite

Apatite is a gem that is a bluish-green hue. Unlike most gems, it is best to store this one by itself because it is soft and easily damaged. This stone is usually used for spells that lead to people having greater wisdom or searching for the truth. It is associated with several parts of the chakra— heart, solar plexus, throat, or crown. Accordingly, it combines different parts of your being to provide further clarity and wisdom. It can be useful when you are meditating or it can help reduce your anxiety if you carry it with you. It can also help you in pursuits that require you to uncover unfound truths by magnifying your intuition and cosmically leading you to answers. Apatite can be used with clear quartz, amethyst, or rose quartz.

Aquamarine

Aquamarine is another blue crystal with greenish tones. It is known for helping people who are feeling worried or who have fears, but it can also be a powerful protection crystal. It is a crystal that tends to amplify, and it is associated with the heart, third-eye, and throat chakras. Therefore, it helps people calm down, feel braver, and have a better understanding of their spiritual selves. It works well with turquoise, clear quartz, and amethyst.

Black Tourmaline

Black Tourmaline is a gem that absorbs energies. Thus, it is great to take around with you if you need protection from negative forces because it will absorb those negative energies rather than sending out good ones to reduce the impact of the bad ones. If you break this gem, you should bury it in the Earth and get a new one so that the negative energy doesn't influence you. This black crystal can be used with clear quartz, and it is associated with the root chakra. Consequently, it is one of the crystals that is most linked with your Earthly connection and your physical body.

Tourmaline can also come in other colors (such as a pink and green color) that are beautiful and can be used in similar fashions to tourmaline, but those will have other chakras based on their color. I love watermelon tourmaline, which is great if you want to manifest a romantic relationship (or for platonic love as well).

Bloodstone

This crystal is sometimes known as heliotrope, and it is a brownish-green color, although it does have various shades that may differ slightly and include specs of red or gold. It was named for a Christian story about the crucifixion of Jesus Christ. It is said that Jesus's blood dropped on green stones, which was said to explain the red specks sometimes found in bloodstone. For Wiccans, it is used to help practitioners move past their negative emotions so that they can unveil the truth and gain the wisdom that they need to help them through their difficult situations. Thus, this stone is perfect when you need to make a decision, and when you feel lost in your emotions.

Carnelian

Carnelian is part of the quartz family, and it is a type of chalcedony. This stone is commonly linked to bravery, and it can help you resist your weaknesses and improve upon them. This crystal is absorbent of energy, and it is associated with the root and sacral chakras. Thus, it is ideal when you need to accomplish tasks that make you feel petrified, when you need to add more passion to your relationships, or when you need to discover who you are. This gem can be used with sardonyx, malachite, or clear quartz.

Chalcedony

This stone is part of the quartz family, and is generally a light blue color. It is called the "speaker's stone," because it allows you to say what you need to say and enunciate your points better. Chalcedony amplifies energy, and it is associated with the throat chakra.

Citrine

Citrine is another one of the most important gems that you will encounter. It is usually yellow, but it is an incredibly translucent yellow. It can either be created or is sometimes naturally occurring. This gem amplifies energy, and it is associated with the solar plexus chakra. Witches commonly place this around their home to create a better home atmosphere. It is known for bringing prosperity, boosting self-confidence, helping with manifestation, and creating a generous spirit. You can place citrine in the corners of your rooms to ensure that you have good energies in your homestead.

Danburite

This crystal comes in many colors that are associated with various chakras. All danburite varieties are linked to being spiritually aware and finding a connection with your higher power. It comes in shades of gray, green, or clear. Green is associated with the heart while the others are associated with the crown. This gem can facilitate unconditional love, make changes easier, reduce stress, cleanse the spaces it is in, and being a high vibration crystal, it can help you connect with the God and the Goddess. Further, you can use this stone with other stones that have high vibrations such as moldavite or phenacite.

Emerald

Emerald is well-known by jewelers, but it is also a vital gem for witches. Witches can buy polished gemstones or they can buy rawer versions of the gem for their practice. This gem is known for its breathtaking green color, and it is a form of beryl, which is a mineral that also makes gems like aquamarine or morganite. Emerald is linked to the heart chakra, which is why it is commonly worn as jewelry, and it is associated with romantic success, unconditional love, and divine love. It is also known as a great gem for protection, recovering from trauma, having spiritual awareness, being kind, and forgiving others. It works well with pink stones, green stones, clear quartz, or other beryls. Emerald is one of my favorite gems because it represents many elements, such as love, kindness, and romance, that I value most.

Epidote

Epidote, like emerald, is a green gem that is linked to the heart chakra. It represents many of the same qualities as the emerald, and it is known for being used between partners to balance their love and effectuate growth between them. This is an amplifying gem, and it is great for healing broken relationships. It can be used with any amplifying stones. Additionally, for people who live in urban areas, this stone is a great choice if you feel like you need more connection to nature.

Fuchsite

This is yet another green gem that is linked to the heart chakra. It is also an absorbing gem. Most commonly, it is used with the ruby to amplify the ruby's power. Frequently, it is worn in a piece of jewelry. This stone is known for its ability to protect and heal. It is a rejuvenating stone and allows growth to come from what has wilted. It is a soft crystal, so you may want to store it separately from your other crystals.

Fluorite

Fluorite is another one of the most common gems that witches use. It is fascinating because of the wide range of colors that it comes in. You can see it in green or purple, and the best type of fluorite for magic is probably the rainbow fluorite that has a variety of colors in it. It is associated with several chakras— throat, crown, third-eye, and heart. It is a great gem to use if you feel the distance between your body and your spirit. Further, it is great for interacting with divine entities, and it can help you bring harmony into your life.

Garnet

Garnet comes in a variety of colors, usually autumn colors like red, yellow, and orange. Garnets amplify energy, and they are associated with different chakras based on their color. Red is associated with the root chakra, green garnets are associated with the heart chakra, and the others are associated with the sacral chakra. Garnets are used for witches to expand their ideas and to prevent themselves from becoming limited. They are also good for benefitting your career. You can use garnets with other colored garnets, and you can use them with both clear and smoky quartz. They are transitional gems, so they are also great when you are going through a period of change.

Howlite

Howlite is a gemstone that is often colored turquoise, but in its natural form, it is mostly colorless or has very little color. This crystal is known for its association with divine entities. It can be used to feel more aligned with the divine. Being a crystal that absorbs, it will take in bad energies, especially overwhelming feelings like anger. It is associated with the crown chakra, and it can be used in correspondence with amethyst and turquoise.

Hematite

Hematite is one of the essential gemstones that I suggest you have in your collection. It absorbs energy, and it is a black stone that will have other colors that run through it, which you can see when you put it in the light. This stone is great when you need to detoxify from negative energies, and it is also great for when you are feeling stressed or like you are ungrounded. It pairs well with either malachite or lapis lazuli.

Jade

Jade is a lovely gemstone that has been long used for its helpful properties. It was even used in ancient times. Jade is known for being green, but it can also come in other hues like orange or white. You have to be careful with jade stones because this crystal is often reproduced, so you must be sure to find genuine jade. Jade absorbs energy, and it is associated with several chakras based on the colors that you have it in. The most common color, green, is related to the heart, but other colors are associated with the root (gray, black, or red), sacral (orange), solar plexus (yellow), crown (white), or third eye (purple). Jade is ideal if you have negative, recurring thoughts that you need to break, and it is good when you need to calm your guilty conscience. Further, it can help your life force and decrease your greed. Finally, it is great for spells regarding love, of any kind. It pairs well with other colors of jade, malachite, and clear quartz.

Jasper

While you might not have heard of this crystal before, it is highly beneficial to have in your collection. Jasper is formed by the combination of different stones like quartz or chalcedony. It comes in a wide range of colors and forms, and it a stone that absorbs energy. Its chakras are linked based on the color that it is. Jasper is the following chakras: third-eye or throat (blue), heart (green), solar plexus (brown or yellow), sacral (orange), or root (red). This stone is excellent for people with mental health issues because it is good for when you have too much energy that results in negative behaviors like eating disorders, addiction, obsessive-compulsive disorder, or anxiety. It can be used with other colors of Jasper, or it can be used with black tourmaline.

Jet

Jet is another lesser-known "crystal" that can have heaps of influence on you and your life. Technically, a jet is not a stone, but it is an honorary one in the world of witchcraft. It is actually pieces of driftwood that have become fossils. Nevertheless, it has long been used to better the well being of people. It is a transmuting stone because it started as wood and then became another substance. This gem can help you stay clearheaded, and it allows you to find mental clarity even in the most chaotic of situations. It is one of the best stones that you can use if you are feeling overwhelmed by grief or sadness. It is also good for protecting your house from harmful spirits and other negative energies.

Kyanite

This brittle crystal is usually found in blue, but it also comes in other shades. Kyanite is frequently shaped to look like a blade, and it is special in that it holds no energy, so you will never need to cleanse it. It is mostly related to the throat chakra, and it can be used to break the stagnancy of your life and to forge new opportunities for you or your loved ones. If you feel stuck in place, kyanite is a great option to get you back on track. It is also great for promoting healthy communication and dependability. You can use it with other colors of kyanite or with you can use it to transfer energy from one crystal to another.

Labradorite

Labradorite is a stone that looks like a normal rock often, but it can shine when it is polished and cut. It looks like moonstones, and First Nation people believed that it connected the earth plane to the other planes of existence. It is associated with the third eye or the throat chakras. Thus, it can be good for enhancing magical attributes, lessening the bad parts of your personality, helping you cleanse yourself of things that you are addicted to, and can help you act less impulsive. Most importantly, perhaps, you can use this to connect with realms other than the Earth realm. You can use this stone in conjunction with amethyst, sodalite, or clear quartz.

Lapis Lazuli

Lapis Lazuli is another object that isn't technically a crystal, but it does have attributes that make it similar to a crystal, and it has been used as a crystal for centuries. This rock absorbs energy, and it is often blue. It is connected to the throat, and it is associated with communication of all kinds. It was even found in the tomb of King Tutankhamen! This can be used with other gems like malachite.

Malachite

Malachite is a vital crystal that many witches like to keep handy. This is a green crystal that absorbs energy. Like many other green crystals, it is associated with the heart chakra. It is known for its association with travel, and it can be used to help you feel more self-assured when you are going to unknown places. It is also useful for blocking pollutants and protecting you from unforeseen incidents. Many witches like to carry this with them when they get on a plane or other modes of transportation. You can use this with lapis lazuli.

Moonstone

Moonstone is a milky stone that is usually white or black. It can help you form bonds with the divine and your intuition. Further, it protects you through amplifying goof energy. It is also great for when you need a creative solution to a problem that you have. Moonstone is associated with the third eye or the crown. It can be used harmoniously with either amethyst or rose quartz.

Onyx

Another black gem is onyx, and it is a type of chalcedony. This stone absorbs energy, and Wiccans commonly associate it with the root chakra. It is linked with sexuality, so it can be used to better your sexual or romantic relationships. It is good to ensure that any excess sexual feelings are balanced, and it reduces the friction in relationships. Further, it is useful if you need more self-control. You can use this gem with carnelian. It is common for Wiccans to put this gem near their beds to maintain their sexual relationships and to keep nightmares at bay.

Peridot

Peridot is a green gemstone that represents many critical emotional areas such as mercy, love, and passion. Peridot is associated with the heart chakra and amplifies romantic energies.

If you would like to be more forgiving, peridot is perfect for you. Further, it can make you feel more compassion for others while reducing your ego. It is an excellent gemstone if you want to ease your traumas and balance your chakras. With peridot, you can cleanse your aura and create more harmony in your life. It is also a great luck booster! You can use peridot in conjunction with any type of quartz.

Quartz Crystal

Quartz crystal, or clear quartz, is perhaps the most important crystal of all for many witches. It is often the crystal that beginner Wiccans start with because it has the most possibilities, and it can be used in a myriad of ways. One of the perks of this crystal is that it will cleanse itself, and it can be used to cleanse other crystals as well (more on cleansing later). This crystal is an amplifier, and it can be used with pretty much any crystal to make the other crystal more powerful. This reasoning is why it's probably the most vital crystal in a witch's collection if you were to rate the importance of the crystals (which I generally don't like to do). It is mostly associated with the crown, but it has connections to all the other chakras as well, which feeds its versatility.

Clear quartz is an excellent gem for connecting to the divine as well as other planes of existence. Further, it can be used to cleanse other objects you are using for your spells. It also is known for providing mental clarity to witches by harmonizing the connection between your body and your mind. Accordingly, it is great to use when you meditate or to keep around you so that you constantly have an object of clarity nearby. The use of clear quartz is nearly endless, and you can use it instead of several more specific crystals when you are in a pinch. If you need an all-purpose crystal, this is perfect. Because it pairs well with all other crystals, it will never interfere with your spells to have clear quartz around.

Rhodochrosite

Rhodochrosite is one of the crystals that I find to be the most beautiful. It is a vibrant pink stone that you could think was rose quartz in its lighter forms, but rhodochrosite usually is more intense in its color, and it has white stripes on it. This crystal amplifies energy, and you can link it to the root and the heart chakras. It is associated with love and kindness. You can also use it to purify your aura. Further, not only does it help you love others, but it helps you to have more compassion for yourself as well, so if you are struggling to love yourself, this gem is ideal for you. You can use it with either clear or rose quartz to add to its power.

Rose Quartz

Rose quartz is another type of quartz that Wiccan witches commonly use. It represents similar ideas as rhodochrosite, such as kindness and love. It is associated with the heart chakra, as many pink stones are, and it is suitable for healing pains related to lost love, such as death or a breakup. By amplifying energy, this stone can help link you with other people and deepen the compassion that you have for them. It can also give you more inner peace and help you be more lighthearted, even in the face of grief. You can use rose quartz with many other crystals like peridot, amethyst, and clear quartz.

Ruby

Ruby is a crystal that comes in vibrant red colors. Like sapphires, a ruby is a version of corundum. Rubies are associated with the chakras of root and heart, and they are linked to all things regarding the heart. They can facilitate divine love. They can also help you get through the more challenging parts of love. For example, they can help you be more emotionally intimate, and they can help you better show your love to your loved ones. Rubies also allow you to embrace feelings that you have tried to repress and ignore, and they will enable you to become more content with those feelings. You can use rubies with rose quartz and sapphires.

Sapphire

Sapphire is a gemstone that many people know, but they often don't realize the amazing attributes that it has. Sapphires can come in many colors, but they are most commonly known for being blue. The blue form represents the third eye or the throat while the pink represents the third eye, the orange represents the sacral, and the yellow represents the solar plexus. The sapphire allows you both to manifest and to protect yourself. It is also great to help you better express yourself and be candid about your feelings. It also helps you relinquish control so that you can let the divine take over and fill you with courage and skill. You can use the sapphire with a ruby.

Sodalite

Sodalite is a blue gem that you can use to amplify energies that you want to be more prominent parts of yourself. This crystal allows you to balance energy so you do not have too much or too little of anything. These gems are great for people who have trouble balancing their moods. It is excellent to use this gem with amethyst.

Smoky Quartz

Smoky quartz is a type of quartz that is used less than clear quartz and rose quartz. Nevertheless, it is still valuable. Smoky quartz turns negative energy into positive energy via transmutation. Smoky quartz usually looks to be gray or brown, and it is associated with the root or crown chakra. You can use it whenever you need to instill more positive energy into your life. It works well with amethyst, clear quartz, and citrine.

Tiger's Eye

Tiger's eye has one of the most intriguing names of all crystals. It is named because it actually looks like the eye of a tiger. It absorbs energy, and you can find it in three colors: red, yellow, and blue. The red is related to the root, the yellow is associated with the solar plexus, and the blue is associated with the throat. You can connect this crystal to all things about the self. If you have a problem with yourself, this is the gem you would want to use. It can help you find self-love and to stop having so much self-criticism.

Further, it can help you create self-compassion and build self-compassion. If you feel lost and don't know who you are, it will help you build a sense of self so that you can have self-worth and self-esteem. It works well with citrine. For health reasons, you should try to use tiger's eye that has been polished because it contains asbestos, which can be harmful if you aren't careful. When it is polished, the asbestos is gone.

Topaz

Topaz is an amplifying gem that comes in several colors, most notably gold or brown, but also is commonly blue. It can be related to the sacral part of you, but based on the color can also be related to the root, the third eye, the solar plexus, the throat, the heart, or the crown. Like tiger's eye, you can use it to help you with yourself and things like self-esteem and expression.

Turquoise

Turquoise is another great crystal. Initially, it served as an essential crystal for soldiers, and it was said to protect warriors from harm. Today, it is still a protective crystal that many use when they need power for themselves and their safety. It's also suitable for protecting relationships and dealing with all kinds of fights. Personal battles and public battles are both issues that you can improve with turquoise. It absorbs energy, and it is a bluish-green color that links it to the throat chakra. You can use it with onyx or clear quartz.

Beyond these crystals listed, there are many more that can have various properties, but these are the major ones that are used by Wiccans and other witches in crystal magic, but you should not limit yourself to just these. Explore your different avenues once you are better established as a crystal practitioner, but for now, these crystals give you the understanding you need as a beginner practitioner.

Crystal Systems

Crystals all have different properties not only by what kind of stone they are and what color they are but also because of how they are shaped. Take note of the shapes of crystals and what those shapes mean to better understand how you can use your crystals to the fullest. While you don't need to know too in-depth what these groups entail, it helps to have a general idea of the classifications of crystals, especially when you start preparing to buy crystals and compare them.

Hexagonal crystals are known for manifestation powers. Meanwhile, isometric crystals are known for bettering hardships, and they also tend to amplify energy. Orthorhombic crystals are cleansing, and triclinic crystals keep bad energies away. Amorphous crystals have dynamic properties. Tetragonal crystals attract other things. Further, trigonal crystals are food for manifestation and protection. Finally, the monoclinic group is good for your intuition.

Hexagonal crystals include beryl, dolomite, quartz, and cinnabar. Isometric crystals include garnet, fluorite, lapis lazuli, and sodalite. Orthorhombic crystals include peridot, iolite, and olivine. Triclinic crystals include turquoise and kyanite. Amorphous minerals include jet and amber. Tetragonal crystals include Zircon, idocrase, and scapolite. Trigonal crystals include rubies and sapphires. The monoclinic system includes moonstone and malachite.

If you don't have certain stones that a spell calls for, you can swap them out for other similar stones that have similar properties and purposes. Use your best judgement and you will probably still have stellar results. Many stones have overlap in their functions, so don't be too rigid with your uses of the stones and try to discover as many ways that they can be used as possible. The more you explore crystal magic, the more clearly you'll see that what crystals you have doesn't matter as much as how you use them because it is your power that taps into the magical qualities crystals possess. It is not their powers that fuel you.

Preparations
Obtaining Crystals

When you first start out, it can be overwhelming to see the long list of crystals that you could buy. Crystals can be expensive, and if you are on a budget, you may think that you'll never be able to do crystal magic. Fear not, though, that is not the case. You don't need to be rich or have an extensive crystal collection to be successful. The truth is that having just one crystal is a great starting point, and it can help you figure out the direction that you'd like to go in next. It's better to buy your crystals slowly, anyway, because then, you will have time to dedicate to each stone that you bring into your home. A connection with crystals is paramount, as you will learn more about throughout this chapter.

If you can find a Wiccan or New Age store, you will be able to easily find the crystals and the other supplies that you may need. There are also sometimes stores that specifically sell crystals, but don't worry. If you don't have a shop nearby, there are several online stores that you can easily find. I prefer to show in person because then you can better feel what crystals you feel drawn to, but with some time and effort, you can work with any crystal that you have and build a connection with the crystals. The most important part is getting a crystal to start magic with and then building the connection with it because that's how you will benefit most from crystal magic.

You don't need to stress yourself out over obtaining crystals. There are plenty of avenues that you can take to find them, and you can determine what feels best for you in the process. You don't need to dive in 110% right away. Ease yourself into buying crystals and respond to what feels right. Let it happen as organically as possible because the better energies that you put into obtaining your crystals, the better you get out in my experience. When in doubt, let your instincts guide you. Try to get in touch with yourself, the Earth, and the divine to find the right crystals for you. Also, look for crystals that will best solve the predominant trouble areas of your life and then expand from there. Alternatively, focus on the crystals that are most predominantly used and paired with other crystals. You'll do just fine if you keep calm.

Tips for the Overwhelmed

So, I've given you an overview of how to get going on purchasing crystals, but many of you still probably feel overwhelmed. You're probably thinking, "Okay, but how do I even know where to start?" My suggestion is to start with a web search. Even if you plan on going to an in-person store, it can help prevent you from being overwhelmed if you have an idea of what options you'll have when you get to the store. You can start to look over prices and shapes to see what appeals to you. Just a little research can go a long way in making you feel more self-assured about your purchases.

Before you even look for crystals, you can cast a spell to ensure that you find good crystals in your search. You can formulate your intentions and speak what you want into existence. You may supplement your intentions by lighting a candle as you repeat what you want. Alternatively, you could make herbal potions that bring good luck and help you become more aligned with the Earth and the divine. Whatever magic you choose to do can help you create a balance that allows a better shopping experience as you choose crystals for the first time.

When you are shopping in person, feel free to stop thinking and instead let the magic happen. See what crystals you feel connected to, and if you can, put them in your dominant hand, and see how you feel when you are holding that crystal. Breathe in and let the energy of that crystal into your body. See how your physical and emotional selves respond to the crystal. Don't overthink it. Just use your feelings to determine whether that feels right. If you're shopping online, you won't have the same information to identify if the crystal feels right to you, but you can still try to look at the pictures and see what reactions they cause in you. Do your best to gauge your response to the crystals, but you can only do as much you can, so don't worry too much when you're shopping.

You're probably tabulating the money in your bank account, wondering how far that money, or lack thereof, will go. When you start to shop, there will be even more options than you dreamed there would be. Some of the crystals will come in lovely shapes, some will be raw, and some will be polished! The fancy pieces will be more expensive, so keep that in mind when you're planning on what you want to purchase and budgeting. Having a basic budget regarding how much you want to spend and on what can help you stay on track and focus your shopping. Also, keep in mind that how a crystal looks won't impact its magic. If you get something shaped nicely, it will work just the same as something that isn't, so if you don't have the budget, don't feel the need to buy the prettiest gems. If you do have the budget, by all means, buy whatever crystals call to you!

Look for smaller crystals when you are shopping. By looking for smaller crystals, you can save a lot of money, and you can save a lot of storage space too, if that is a concern of yours. Large gems can be great if you have space and money for them, but small ones can be so cost-effective, and they can easily be carried around as talismans if you are so inclined. Just like smoother stones don't work better than natural ones, bigger stones don't work better than smaller ones. The magic is in what you do with the crystals, not what the crystals look like, so don't get caught up in trying to get the biggest and most expensive things if doing so feels burdensome.

Don't buy everything all once. You need to be able to handle your crystals and put the energy required into using them. Buying so many crystals at once, not only is expensive, but it can be hard for you to pay attention to the crystals as they need. It's better to start with one or just a few so that until you get used to working with stones, you can direct your full attention to them to ensure that you are successfully incorporating them into your life. Magic isn't a race. You don't need to do everything right away. Work at a pace that makes you feel comfortable because it's better to do good quality work than a higher quantity of work when it comes to magic. You need to build a bond with your stones. It's kind of like a relationship, so imagine trying to make fifteen friends all at once! That's a lot harder than making fifteen friends one by one.

You don't have to buy anything new if you don't want to. However, new crystals are easier to find. You can obtain crystals in a myriad of ways. You might find secondhand crystals, or you may even find some yourself. Alternatively, some may be given as gifts. Accept the crystals as they come your way. Sometimes, some of the best crystals are the ones that you weren't looking for. They are the ones that unexpectedly come into your life and make you feel drawn to them organically. That feeling is one of the best that a Wiccan can feel. Sometimes, you just know. Don't fight that feeling.

It's okay to be a little stressed at first. I want you to stay as calm as possible, but if these new things make you feel a bit anxious, that's acceptable. You don't need to try to ignore the concerns you have. Instead, try to embrace them and work through them because by doing that, you will be in a better headspace to deal with the magic you are creating. Know that nothing happens overnight. It will take a while before you are fully incorporated into the Wiccan world, and even when you are, you'll still have learning to do. You will never stop learning, and that's part of the fulfillment of Wicca.

Let yourself make mistakes. You're not going to get everything perfect, so don't try. Let yourself try your best and be open to the mistakes you make. When you make mistakes, learn from them. You might buy one crystal and realize that you would rather another style. That's okay. You can still appreciate the crystal you have and save up to get the one that really appeals to you. No matter what you do, you will make mistakes, but don't let those mistakes force you into quitting something that is so rewarding when you exert the required energy.

When crystals come your way, be sure to be grateful and give thanks to your deities for their role in locating your crystals. Remember that the crystals are yours to have and that you are going to form a special connection with them. Embrace that connection. Let it fill you and let it better your magic. Enjoy the crystals as new parts of your life, and let good energies surround you. The crystals will bring good things if you believe in their power and harness it. Sometimes, you may want to give your old crystals to other people. When this happens, you may feel an intuitive sense that the crystals belong somewhere else. Alternatively, you may feel that they are drawn back to the Earth, and you can return them to the ground and let them be one with the Earth again.

Getting Acquainted with Your Crystals

It may seem silly to you, but you need to get to know your crystals. You have to listen to them and know what their wants are. You have to create a relationship with them, just like you would create a relationship with anything else in your life. The crystals all have unique energies. Even two crystals of the same kind can have incredibly different energies, so you have to pay attention to the energies of each crystal. Crystals need attention or they won't do anything for you! Let them become a part of your life rather than placing them aside and hoping that they will do something.

Before you try to use the energy of the crystal, I want you to hold it and take in its energies. Learn what it makes you feel and try to form a connection between it and you. It will serve you well to take some time to learn about your new crystals before you five into using them in spells. Before you do anything else, you should feel like you have a closeness to your crystals. Some crystals will connect with you more quickly than others. For example, I felt almost immediately connected to a stone given to me by my grandmother because of the emotional establishments already formed. You need to feel a level of closeness to all your crystals so that they can work properly.

You probably don't want to wait before you start doing spells with your crystals, but being patient is an important part of Wiccan magic. You have to put the work in before you can get any reward. Magic is all about being attuned to your surroundings and the natural and spiritual parts of Earth. Accordingly, nothing worthwhile is going to happen if you don't let those crucial connections form. Having to form a bond with your crystals should feel like something meditative and rewarding rather than like a chore. If it feels like a chore, you're in the wrong mindset for magic. You need to address any negative mindset that you may have if you want to be successful.

Cleansing Your Crystals

When you get your crystals, you are going to have to cleanse them. Likely, they have been handled by several other people before you, which means that those crystals are polluted with bad or distracting energies that will detract from your magic. The different energies aren't likely to harm you, but you still want to get rid of them so that your own energy is entirely in the crystal, and there are no little hiccups in your magic. Purifying your crystals also helps you establish a connection to them because they become your vessels and are connected fully to you and your magic.

You can clean your stones in whatever way that you desire. The easiest way to do this is probably just to wash your stone with water while repeating a purity spell such as, "Clear away the tainted energy of the hands and hearts that touched this gem before me." Your spell, of course, doesn't have to rhyme. It doesn't have to sound pretty, but some people like to carefully craft their words because they feel more empowered that way. Spells can be whatever you make them, so make them yours and embrace them. When you use water, be careful with soft gems and simply put small amounts of water on them so that they don't get destroyed. Be aware of the needs of your crystals during this process.

Another way to cleanse a crystal is to simply hold it in your hand under moonlight, light a candle, and cast a spell. The combination of these three actions is the way that I have found best cleanses the crystals for me. I usually use the incantation, "Under this your moon, Goddess, I hold this piece of Earth tenderly, hoping that it will guide me through the hardships and wonders that I will face. As the wax melts, melt away the polluted energies from this stone I hold dearly, and let the dim moonlight be one with the flame, so I can charge this stone with my own tongue of energy." Again, you can use whatever spell feels useful to you. During the new and full moon are ideal for cleansing your crystals, but you can cleanse them anytime that you please.

There are other ways that you cleanse your crystals, such as using incense or burying your stones under dirt in your yard for a while to connect them to Earth. Whatever cleansing spell you can think of will work as long as your intentions are strong. Use whatever calls to you to cleanse your stones. Sometimes, you may feel the need to use several distinct methods to accomplish your goals. Every so often, you'll want to repeat the cleansing process because they need refreshing every so often because of negative energies that may pass through them or mishandling by other people. Continue to take care of your crystals as long as they are yours. Ensure that they are cleansed and ready for the spells that you would like to use them for by tending to the crystals as they require.

Crystals will lose their luster if you do not care for them. They will not be as strong if you aren't sure to tend to them, so be sure that you always keep them in top shape, just as you would your car or your home or anything else that you valued.

Charging Crystals

When you have magic tools, they require charging. Just like your phone or laptop needs charging before you can do any work with them, so do magical tools. Of course, the charging with magical tools is done in a very different way, but the point is that when you plan to use things for magic, you have to put energy inside of them so that you can channel that energy through your spell. Different Wiccans have various stances on how this energy works and the nuanced details, but it is universal that making sure things contain good energy is important.

Beyond just charging your stones for spells, it is good to charge them anyway because even without a spell, having them around can improve your life, and they can send and absorb energy without you even having to tell them to do so. Because they are entities that naturally contain energy, they are going to deal with energy whether you charge them or not. Still, when you charge your objects, you are controlling the energy that is inside of them, which is what gives you so much power.

Keep in mind that when you charge things, you'll want to charge them in ways that reflect that item's power. Crystals have different properties, and when you keep those properties in mind while charging your items, you can better dictate how those crystals will be used when it comes time to cast a spell. Rose quartz is not the same as jade, and you shouldn't treat it as such. Just like you wouldn't like to be treated like another human because you're different, crystals need to be treated with different attitudes when being charged as well.

To charge your crystals, you can go about it in several ways. You can use the moonlight or the sunlight to charge your crystals as you cleanse them. You can also use methods such as sprinkling them with herbs or ringing a bell around them. Like always, your intentions are the most critical part of your charging because it is from your own power that you are spreading energy to the crystals. You can also customize your charging method to what you plan to use the crystal for. For example, if you want to use it for psychic intuition, the moon is a good source because it is connected to spiritual and psychic parts of you. Alternatively, if you're looking for balance, you can use herbs or soil to charge your crystals.

Aim to charge your crystals right after you have cleansed them so that they have not yet absorbed other energies and remain pure. Generally, if you are using a crystal in a spell, you should charge it for what you are doing again, even if you have charged it before, so that your charge reflects your intentions. When you charge it in this case, you can hold it in your hand and imagine your magical energy going into the crystal and feel it becoming linked to you. When using a crystal for spells, charge them right before you begin the spell.

Charging crystals, or any other magical devices, is a crucial part of spellwork and witchcraft. You want to be sure that the right energies and intentions are going into your crystals so that you can get the best results. The more you practice charging your crystals, the easier it will get. You may feel a little lost right now, but it is one of those processes that is best learned through experience because it is so individual. It is hard to go wrong when you charge your item, so if you're following your intuition and doing what feels right for your purposes, you probably are doing just fine. If you're part of a coven, you will likely have a community that can help you. Otherwise, there are also several online forums you can join that can give you more personal insight.

Creating Crystal Magic

The following instructions will give you a starting point for your magic. You can create your own spell and magic as you get more advanced. Still, beginners often like to be told what to say, so here are some fundamental crystal and incantation combinations that you use to make positive changes in areas that you struggle with the most. You can use crystals for almost any problem that you have, and here are only a few examples of the combinations you can use.

Protection

If you are feeling unsafe and would like an easy spell for protection, you can use black tourmaline as an excellent crystal that provides stability and security.

Light a black candle*, which is known for being protective, and read the following incantation with the black tourmaline in your hand.

At times, the world feels so unsafe. I feel doom upon me, breathing down my neck and trying to inundate me, but I won't let the pains and torments catch me as I go through life the best I can and try to survive. God and Goddess, let this black tourmaline protect me, so I can serve the Earth in the ways that you intend, and I can feel secure in the life I have ahead.

When you have finished the incantation, blow the candle out, and then, you may place the gem somewhere unique to you or in a place that you feel needs the most protection.

*If you do not have a black candle, you can use a white candle because in Wicca tradition, because white contains all the colors, it can be swapped for anyone color if you need it to be.

Positivity

To be more positive, you can also use the combination of a black candle, which keeps negativity away and a crystal. Follow the same protocols as above, but swap out the crystal and the incantation. Use lapis lazuli for your crystal because it helps you acknowledge the positivity even when life doesn't go to plan. Further, you can use the following incantation.

Life does not always go the way I hope, but I want to take the goodness in because I feel it around. Let the hope rush through this crystal and into me. Let the positivity begin, so I don't have to continue to worry about all the things that I cannot control.

Guilt

Peridot can be used to help you relieve your guilt. It can help you remember to love yourself again.

I am free from the guilt because I have learned that I am human, and I can only strive to do the best that I can. Now, I am learning to harbor more positive energy.

Place the peridot in a potion of lavender (either from a plant of essential oils), and tea. Mix in the petals of a flower that you love for added potency and a touch of something that is important to you. Write the thing you are guilty of on a small piece of paper and put that into the mix as well.

As you mix the potion, repeat the incantation several times. You can remove the crystal from the potion. Alternatively, you can leave it in and keep the crystal in the potion for a while and let it serve as a reminder and magical item for a week or so.

Anxiety or Stress

If you are feeling anxious or stressed, using a combination of amethyst and rose, quartz can really improve your mental state and help you feel calm.

Take the gems in your hands, one in each hand, and begin an incantation.

These gems I carry with me will keep the worry from my mind, so the weight that's on my shoulders can flee my body and give me the chance to focus on better things that will help me achieve all that I want to make real.

Keep the gems close to you to ward off anxiety. If there's something specific that is bothering you, you can add that item into the incantation and call it by name.

Anger

If you are feeling like you are struggling to control your anger and have too much of it building up in your body, howlite is a great choice to help you reduce your anger. You can carry it with you to help yourself keep a level head in stressful situations that may make your anger kick into high gear.

Light a red candle, and let it burn as you begin your incantation.

With the light of this candle, I will use the howlite to channel my rage and let it burn swiftly before it can consume me.

Blow out the candle, and then continue the incantation, picking up the stone with your non-dominant hand.

Let all the anger be absorbed into this crystal. Take the rage I feel and let it melt to calmness. Let the calm be my guide going ahead. Let this crystal look out for me.

Love

If you are dealing with lost love, wanting to repair hurting love, or are looking to find love to break through your loneliness, this is the spell for you.

In this spell, you are going to use both a ruby and rose quartz. You should start by laying down. Place the ruby and the rose quartz over your chest. Then, repeat your incantation as many times as you need.

I have been hurt by love before, but I want to try to bring the love back to me. I want to feel it in my heart and let the joy of love fill my whole body. I am lonely now, staying on my own, but there is someone out there who can fill my heart in the painful spots where these love magnifying crystals rest. These gems will remind me to keep my heart open to the love that could find me.

Mental Illness

You can use crystals to help you deal with your mental illnesses. As you know, many crystals deal with stress and anxiety, and several others also have the power to help you control addiction, eating disorders, and OCD as well.

My mind is burdened by an ailment that I cannot control. I feel powerless to my behaviors, but I do not have to give in to the forces that try to destroy me. I can use my energy to build a new start and heal my broken parts— both physical and mental.

Hold a jasper crystal in your non-dominant hand, knowing that this crystal can help you because it takes excess energy and balances it. It absorbs all the bad energies, and it allows you to become lighter mentally as a result. This crystal will allow you to resist negative impulses that come with mental illness and help you make choices that will benefit you rather than relieve your mental pain only momentarily. You may struggle, but in the end, you will come out ahead. Repeat the incantation several times until you feel that you and the crystal are starting to become linked and that your energy is radiated into that crystal.

When you finish the incantation, place the crystal somewhere that is relevant to your mental illness. For example, if you have OCD and like to brush your teeth compulsively, place the crystal next to your toothbrush. Alternatively, you could carry the jasper with you to feel its energy as you go about your day. It is up to you to decide where your crystal would be most meaningful.

CHAPTER 6
Beyond What Glimmers

Wiccan crystal magic goes much beyond the glimmering qualities of crystals. There are so many wonderful things combined. While it is easy to look at beautiful crystals like jade or ruby and see how lovely they are, it is much harder to look beyond that beauty and realize all the work and dedication it takes to master crystals and have them work in your favor. You won't just be able to make them work without investing parts of yourself. You need to have faith and believe in your own skills and the power that is inherent in the natural world as well as the divine and spiritual worlds. There is magic all around you, but you need to embrace it. You need to be unafraid of it. You need to let it fuel your skills rather than ignoring it. Accept crystal magic for what it is, and you will have worlds of delight.

Crystal magic is also about the wonder and blessedness of the Wiccan religion. It is a way to celebrate the God, the Goddess, and the Earth that they grace with such blessings. If you would like to be a Wiccan, you have to carry your religious practices and beliefs through all that you do. All your magic must channel the divine and the wonders that the divine brings. Embrace and adore what you the universe has given you, for it is holy. Every part of this earth has an energy that you can use to learn to your advantage. These energies will help you grow spiritually, physically, and mentally. All you have to do is allow them to be part of you. Let them thrive. Let the Wiccan faith guide you and embrace you as you are because Wiccans are open to all the people who have been rejected and disempowered by the rest of the world.

Wiccan crystal magic also incorporates all the amazing facets of witchcraft in ways that inspire and motivate people. It is not just an aimless form of witchcraft that has no organization or no rules. It has parameters while still giving you ample room to explore and figure out you really are. It is a lifestyle that incorporates so many different elements. Crystals are not just rocks to the practitioners who use them. They are not only pieces of jewelry. They are tools that you can use to embrace witchcraft and empower Wiccans to do better work on this earth. Those tools are ones that you too can channel and let them make you part of something bigger than yourself.

It is a way of embracing the magic that people have within all along, and it can be used to celebrate through rites, rituals, festivals, and spells. It is a way of engaging with all the things that Wiccans hold dear. When you practice crystal magic, you are reaching new levels of yourself, but you are also able to be part of a community. You have people who can tell you how to be your best self. Those people can send you in the right direction. Even if you work in solitary, there is a community out there that will welcome you and that you can relate to. There are thousands of Wiccans, and in such an interconnected world, you are never alone. Don't be afraid to spread the magic or reach out to other Wiccans. Being part of a community is the way that magic continues to be shared and handed down through the generations.

You must learn how to use your power for good because that is what Wiccans strive to do. Do not try to use crystal magic for evil because that is not in the spirit of the Wiccan Rede. You need to use your magic in ways that help yourself and the people you love without hurting others in the process. Be merciful and compassionate to others just as you would want others to be to you. Magic requires a great deal of responsibility, but if you remain kind and loving, you won't have to worry about straying from good.

It takes practice and work to build your magical repertoire, but it is nothing that you cannot do. You have so much power in your body and all the things around you. You don't need crystals to do magic, but they are one of the best tools that a witch can ever have. They are beautiful, but they are also so powerful. They allow you to focus on specific tasks and better harness the power that you've had all along. Don't be afraid of crystal magic. It can't hurt you unless you hurt yourself.

Throughout the process, you will learn what makes crystals so unique. It is one thing for me to tell you the magical properties of crystals, but it is much more remarkable for you to experiment and realize the wonders by yourself. Undoubtedly, crystal magic is something that you learn through exploration and experimentation. The more you try, the more you will learn, and the more you will be able to do. When you start to discover crystal magic, you will unlock parts of yourself and the world that you didn't even realize existed. You'll realize that you are so much more than you ever imagined. Through faith and magic, you can find new parts of yourself that are begging for you to awaken via witchcraft. Don't fight the magic within you anymore. Let it be free. Pick up a crystal and let its energy become one with you.

CONCLUSION

You have made it through to the end of the book, and I appreciate that you have made it this far. Thank you so much for reading, and I hope that you have learned the wonders of Wiccan crystal witchcraft. Of course, what you do next is now up to you, but if you enjoyed this book, I urge you to continue to explore all things Wicca and crystal witchcraft because this is only a starting point for the wonders that you can do. Imagine all the amazing feats that you could accomplish if you stay on this path. Witchcraft and Wicca both require practice and time, but when you invest in them, you get so much more in return.

Now that you have finished learning the fundamentals, you now need to put what you have learned into practice. Start with a few of the spells that I have given you. Also, make some spells of your own! Fill up your book of shadows with explorations of your craft, and if you want, join a Wiccan coven to find a community of like minded people who want the same things that you do. Whatever you choose to do going forward, please consider utilizing witchcraft to lessen the issues of your life and to find inner peace.

If this book was at all helpful to you, please leave a review on Amazon. Hopefully, this book has given you the knowledge you need to understand better what Wiccan witchcraft is. Now, go out and buy your first crystal. (I know you want to!)

DESCRIPTION

Wicca Crystal Magic is a straightforward book that will teach you the fundamentals that you need to start becoming a Wiccan, as well as to start Wiccan crystal witchcraft. This book is ideal for people who have just begun Wicca or who want more profound insight into how to combine both Wicca and crystal magic. Even people who have some experience with Wicca and witchcraft can already benefit from the concise and understandable descriptions and spells provided in this book.

Many people automatically assume that the terms Wicca and witchcraft are synonymous, but that couldn't be further from the truth. Wiccan is a religion that uses witchcraft while anyone, religious or not, can use witchcraft. Wicca is so much more than witchcraft, just as witchcraft is so much more than Wicca. Combined, the two areas nicely merge the divine with the supernatural. They allow you to connect to the cosmic forces while still connecting to the Earthly ones and yourself.

This book will give you all you need to know to change your life in ways that you never expected. If you feel stagnated and aren't sure what your purpose is, you can begin to learn who you are through magic and witchcraft. There's no need to continue living life feeling undervalued or out of touch with the natural world. Embrace everything that is around you rather than trying to ignore all the things that could make you stronger. Let yourself grow and welcome the beautiful energies that surround each of us.

In this book, you will:

- Learn what Wicca is and about the history of Wicca
- Be taught the different types of Wicca and how Wicca is different from other forms of witchcraft
- Understand the thirteen principles of Wicca as well as the Wiccan Rede
- Learn about Wiccan rituals and rites as well as the eight major Wiccan festivals
- Receive comprehensive definitions for a myriad of Wiccan and witchcraft terms

- Know how to start creating magic using crystals
- Get easy to understand details about the different crystals Wiccans use and what they can do for you
- Discover Wiccan crystal spells that will help you begin crystal witchcraft
- Start to embrace all that it means to be a Wiccan crystal witch

By the time you have read this book, you will have all the information you need to begin creating real, powerful magic. You will have the knowledge you need to decide whether the Wiccan route is right for you. Using this information, you can unleash new parts of yourself that you've only dreamed of finding. You will be able to take charge of your life, and you will grow as a person—spiritually, mentally, and physically. Everyone dreams of being magical at least sometimes, and through *Wicca Crystal Magic,* you can embrace those dreams while feeling happier and healthier in the process. You'll find a connection to a higher power, which will enable you to be more than just another one of billions of people. You are unique, so let that uniqueness thrive.

TAROT FOR DUMMIES

Learn Tarot Reading Exercises, Tarot Card Meanings, Tarot Spreads, Increase Your Intuition and Master the Art of Tarot

Lisa Miller

INTRODUCTION

Welcome to *Tarot for Dummies*! By purchasing this book, you've decided to go on a fascinating journey through past centuries to learn how to use, read, and interpret one of the world's most well-known divination tools. If you've always wanted to learn to read tarot, then you are definitely in the right place!

In the chapters that follow, you'll learn about the incredible history of the tarot deck, from its origins in gameplay, through its modern uses in prediction and foretelling. Did you know that there are several regional variations of the tarot deck? You'll find out all about those variants in the history chapters at the beginning of the book!

Tarot for Dummies will also give you detailed information on every card in the tarot deck so that you can become well-acquainted with their appearances and meanings. There are chapters on each suit of the deck. Then we'll break the suits down into individual cards so you can familiarize yourself with each one and how its role works with the other cards to make a complete set. You'll also learn the best ways to shuffle, deal, and interpret the deck for the most accurate readings.

Because tarot relies on the reader as much as the cards, you'll also learn about the less technical aspects of tarot, from learning to trust your intuition, perform readings with the purest of intents, and knowing how to read the cards when the deal is less than clear-cut. A tarot reader must be able to have confidence in themselves, the cards, and their interpretations to do justice to the cards and the subject of the reading. Once you've learned these basics, you'll be ready to practice your new skills for your friends, your family, and even some trusting strangers!

That's another thing we'll tackle in this book- how do you handle the skepticism of those who don't believe in the power of the tarot cards? While you want everyone to take your readings seriously, there will always be those who scoff, so make sure to check out the last chapters of the book for ways to tactfully handle all types of people, both believers and non-believers. The intuition you'll need to read your tarot cards often extends into the ability to read people, so you'll want a solid understanding of how to deal with the subjects of your readings, as well as the cards themselves.

If you're ready to put your trust and your intuition to work with a tarot deck, then *Tarot for Dummies* is the only primer you'll need to learn the ins and outs of the cards, their meanings, and how to deal and interpret the cards for maximum effect and accuracy. Come along with us on a journey through the intriguing history of the deck through its modern-day applications to discover how you can use tarot to guide not only the lives of others but your own life, too. Let's get started!

PART I
A History of Tarot

Long before the tarot deck was used as a tool for divination, it was used for other amusements, namely card games, and we still see the legacy of the tarot deck in modern playing cards. Playing cards were introduced into Europe in the latter part of the 14th century, where they underwent several evolutions to develop into the various iterations of playing cards and tarot cards we see today. Let's take a look at how these evolutions occurred over the centuries!

14th Century

The first mention of playing cards in Europe are found after the mid-1370s, and it's likely that they were brought into the major port of Venice from China, Egypt, or India. There's a record that shows that three custom gilded decks of playing cards were purchased by the palace for the amusement of French King Charles VI, who by all accounts suffered from mental illness and required a new pastime to soothe his restlessness.

These early card decks already featured what we recognize today as four 'suits' of 13 cards, numbered with pips from one through ten, with three 'court cards'; at that time, the suits were most commonly called swords, cups, coins, and clubs. The novelty of this amusement spread rapidly through mainland Europe, with records showing that they reached Germany, Spain, and France soon after their introduction in Italy. Games began to be invented to make use of the cards, and regional variations began to spring up.

15th Century

In the 15th century, a new suit was added to the standard 52 card deck, which is still a part of the modern tarot deck. The cards were called 'trionfi' or 'triomphe' cards, which has translated into

English as 'trump.' These cards were meant to be allegorical in nature and depicted scenes with religious significance or of the natural world. There was no standard for how many cards could be in the trump suit, and decks might range from 60 cards (8 added trumps) up to 100 cards. There are very few surviving decks from this time, but the ones that have been discovered were made from the finest materials, mostly expensive hand-painted wood and copper. These decks were commissioned by wealthy families and often featured elaborate portraiture and nature scenes.

As tarot card decks continued their spread across the European continent through the 15th century, innovations in production methods made them more accessible to the wider population. Even the poorest populations were making cards out of waste paper (sadly, very few have stood the test of time). In Italy, where tarot took root the earliest, several games began to emerge using a deck of 78 cards, which would become the basis for the modern tarot deck. These 78 cards were split into 22 trump cards and four suits of 14 cards each, with numbered cards one through ten, and four face cards or court cards- king, queen, knight, and knave (or page).

Variations of this 78-card deck and the Italian game *tarocchi* would find their way into Germany (*tarock*) and France (*jeu de tarot*), as well as Hungary, Austria, and other points north. By the end of the 15th century, tarot cards had become popularized in almost every region of Europe, save the British Isles and the modern-day Balkan states. Tarot was also slow to become mainstream in Spain and Portugal, although it wasn't unheard of to be played there. Versions of all these games are still played across Europe today.

16th Century

The French seemed to take ownership of the tarot deck in the sixteenth century and began to standardize the decks, which are remarkably similar to what we see in both regular playing cards and tarot decks today. Tarot began at this time to move away and distinguish itself from gameplay cards. It was the French who would heavily influence both types of cards and build a 'card game' industry.

By the mid-16th century, gameplay cards made in France would settle into the 52-card deck of four 13-card suits that we are familiar with for most card games today, including the suits themselves- clubs, diamonds, hearts, and spades. While those in the upper class continued to commission personalized hand-made decks, cards for the commoners began to pop up in every corner of France, as materials became cheaper and easier to produce. The card games began to take on the final rules that they continued to be played with; most games that use a tarot deck are trick-taking games that often pair partners like bridge or euchre.

For the tarot deck, a massive change was coming, and the deck that was developed would become the basis for tarot cards for the coming centuries. It was in the late 1500s that a deck emerged called the *Tarot de Marseille,* although this name wasn't applied until much later. This French deck, based on the Italian *Tarocco Piemontese* deck, featured standardized numbered pip cards, one through ten, and four court cards for each suit, as well as 22 trump cards that featured pictures and scenes, numbered one through twenty-two, and one 'fool' card. The suited cards – batons, cups, coins, and swords- are now known as the *Minor Arcana*, and the 22 trump cards are known as the *Major Arcana*.

17th Century

The Tarot de Marseille tarot deck spread back into Italy, where it had originated, and became immensely popular for gameplay. Although small regional variations still existed, the vast majority of commissioned and common tarot decks were in this style. Italians found the artwork on the French-style cards to be intriguing, and in some instances, replaced the Christian religious symbolism with images of the old Roman gods and goddesses. Swiss cards were also known to replace Christian imagery with pagan images, at times drawing the ire of the Catholic church. Larger and smaller decks started to become rarer as the 78-card deck was the most widely produced, and people began to adapt their games to the size of the deck.

18th Century

The first mention of tarot as a divination tool is in a text dated 1750, author unknown, ascribing esoteric meanings to each of the trump cards, as well as the suited cards by number. The art of cartomancy was then born in the drawing rooms of French high society, which would also soon become deeply entrenched in the teachings of Mesmer, the father of modern hypnotism. With the birth of the use of tarot in the occult, the estrangement of the gameplay deck and the tarot deck was complete.

Before we go any farther, let's take a moment to define the word 'occult' because it tends to have negative connotations. From the Latin "occulare"- to conceal, occult simply means something of a supernatural or mysterious origin or something that isn't immediately known to outsiders. For French occultists in the late 18th century, tarot was another tool in the toolbox to determine the unknown or the unseen. Using a Tarot de Marseille deck modified from an Italian *Tarocco Bolognese*, prominent Huguenot cleric and scholar Antoine Court wrote a treatise on the use of tarot as a divination tool. While his essay may not have been historically accurate as to the origin of the imagery on tarot cards, it was his work that set off the cartomancy craze.

Monsieur Court was a fascinating figure, holding fast to his belief that the tarot deck was a 'gift' and holdover from ancient Egypt, although there are no recorded histories to support his theory. Court also held fast to his Protestant faith, despite living and working in predominantly Catholic France. It may be that his Protestantism was considered a more intractable offense than his interest in the occult that saved him from being heavily persecuted. It may have also been his well-cultivated friendships and Freemason associations, including none other than American founding father and fellow Mason Benjamin Franklin. They spent a considerable amount of time in France in the 1780s and 1790s.

Court also attracted the attention of another occultist, who called himself Etteilla, born Jean-Baptiste Alliette. Etteilla (Alliette reversed) countered Court's claims of having invented cartomancy with his published work, a book titled "How to Entertain Yourself with the Deck of Cards Called Tarot." In this book, Etteilla detailed using an occult deck of tarot cards to perform fortunetelling and declared that Court's Egyptian theory was bunk and that he (Etteilla) had been practicing cartomancy as early as 1750.

Etteilla had already been considered a master of card games and card tricks, having made a name for himself in parlors all over France by performing with a piquet deck- the precursor of the modern playing card deck. When he began developing the art of tarot for divination in the late 1770s and early 1780s, his associates were eager to have their cards read using the new tarot method.

Etteilla is also responsible for the modern tarot deck, assigning an esoteric meaning to the 78 cards of the Major and Minor Arcana and redesigning the artwork to incorporate many Egyptian depictions. This was despite Etteilla railing against Court's claims about tarot's Egyptian origin several years before; it would seem the good cartomancer realized that the Egyptian theory was exotic enough to sell his cards and his reading talents. By the time of his death in 1791, he had trained several cartomancy apprentices to follow in his teachings.

While Court's theories on tarot were largely lost to the annals of time, Etteilla's legacy lives on in the modern tarot deck and the mixed opinions that he evokes in cartomancy historians. There are some that praise his innovation in bringing tarot for divination to the masses, while others say he was a sensationalist who ruined the mystical spirit of tarot reading by making it too mainstream.

19th Century

The 1800s were an interesting time for the development of tarot for divination. The students of Court and Etteilla were coming into their own and trying to make their mark on the tarot deck. At the same time, the practices of spiritualism were shedding the constraints of traditional religion, as upper- and middle-class citizens all over Europe were looking for new diversions after the political upheavals of the previous century.

This made for a perfect storm of innovation, spiritual exploration, and a deep belief in the occult. It was also around this time that the British, who had never had an interest in tarot as a card game, began to take note of the cards as a method of divination. Victorian Englanders were heavy into spiritualism and the occult, seeing it as a welcome diversion from the drudgery of everyday life. Some of the most famous British spiritualists include the infamous Aleister Crowley and the much-respected Sir Arthur Conan Doyle, creator of the beloved Sherlock Holmes.

During this time, both French and British students of the tarot began to adapt Etteilla's deck to suit their own purposes. Even while they were changing up the artwork and configurations, the legacy of Etteilla's interpretative meanings and the number of cards, 78, would remain the same. In France, occultists Eliphas Levi and Gerard Encausse were working separately to try to add Hebrew and Kabbalah elements to the tarot deck. The two would also try to incorporate Zodiac signs into the tarot interpretation but to little avail.

While the Frenchmen were trying to add new elements into the deck, in England, an occultist and magician by the name of Samuel Mathers was using tarot as an integral part of his new religious sect, The Hermetic Order of the Golden Dawn. Mathers was a polyglot, a writer, and a devoted believer in the power of the occult. Mathers would be responsible for the final transformation of tarot from a card game to tarot as a divination method. He would take the landmark work that Etteilla had composed and the deck that the Frenchman had created, and move the art and interpretation of the tarot deck into the form that is now what would be considered the first truly modern set of tarot cards.

Mathers is also responsible for the mysticism surrounding the reading of tarot. He believed and taught his followers to believe that tarot has absolute power in reading the future. He also taught that the ability to read the cards obligated the reader to keep the secrets that he interpreted. This air of mystery still surrounds the reading of tarot today. Among the many others who followed Mathers' teachings was Irish poet W.B. Yeats. Yeats would attempt to incorporate Celtic mythology into the tarot deck, and the beautiful artwork this entailed survives into some iterations of the modern tarot.

By the end of the 19th century, many new versions of the tarot deck had emerged, failed, fell into disuse, and faded away. It was the deck that Etteilla had developed in the 18th century that stood the test of development, use, and interpretation. His seminal work truly did lay the groundwork for tarot in mysticism and the occult. Mathers' alterations only stood to strengthen the foundation laid by Etteilla.

20th Century into Present Times

Tarot experienced a tremendous amount of growth and popularity as the 19th century came to a close and the new century began. It was during this period that the 'final' standards of tarot deck came into being, and those are some of the decks we'll focus on for the remainder of the book. Tarot decks can absolutely be personalized to fit your tastes, but since there are endless possibilities, our job is to introduce you to the basics so you can make decisions based on a solid understanding of the fundamentals.

The first deck that we'll outline is the Falconnier-Wegener set. This deck is an Egyptian-style deck that evolved from the teachings of Etteilla and his followers. The artwork was designed by European occultists based on the writings of Paul Christian, who was an avid student of cartomancy as popularized by Etteilla. This deck would go on to become the basis for the illustrations in many pieces of early 20th-century literature about the use of tarot and was used in publications as late as the 1970s. The Falconnier-Wegener set was also among the first to become popular across North America.

It was during the first half of the 1900s that Crowley first published his Thoth deck, and although the artwork and interpretation were widely praised at first, it fell into obscurity around before becoming popular again in the late 1960s. While Crowley was British, many of his followers were American, and societies such as the Hermetic Order of the Golden Dawn and the Ordo Templi Orientis took up the use of the deck in their teachings. Remnants of Crowley's Thoth deck can be seen in the printings of modern decks like the Cosmic Tarot and the Tarot of the Spirit.

The Tarot de Marseille also experienced a brief resurgence in the mid-1900s, but quickly faded away again. In fact, other styles became so much more prominent than the Tarot de Marseille that this venerable grandfather of the modern tarot deck has been all but forgotten. These days, one must do a lot of digging to find a TdM deck, even among online collectors. Those that can find and use them say the decks are beautifully-colored and are easy to use and interpret. Even so, it would seem the ancestor of modern tarot died a death of natural attrition as other decks increased in popularity.

The last deck we'll detail in this section is the deck that we'll use as an example and foundational deck through the remainder of the book, and that's the Rider Waite Smith tarot. Introduced in 1909, the deck was conceived by A.E. Waite, a British member of the Golden Dawn occultist group. He commissioned artist Pamela Coleman Smith to create the illustrations for his deck, paying her a flat fee and leaving her name off the publication- a perceived wrong that modern publishers have chosen to right by adding her name to the deck in subsequent contemporary printings. Although Coleman was also a member of the Hermetic Order of the Golden Dawn, she chose not to use their imagery on the deck, instead opting to study earlier iterations of tarot that she found in museums and private collections.

The resulting deck is a mix of original tarot traditions, Christian imagery, and bit and pieces of Renaissance artwork and Smith's own creativity. The Major Arcana, designed by Waite to be illustrated by Smith, featured a reimagining of previous Egyptian-style art, with a touch of religious symbolism and the teaching of the Golden Dawn. The Minor Arcana was left entirely to Smith's devices, and she used her distinct style of illustration to pay homage to the tarot art of the previous centuries.

The RWS deck, as it came to be known, exploded in popularity in Europe, so much so that it was pirated (yes, media piracy was already a thing!) in 1916 by an American publisher named DeLaurence. The deck and accompanying interpretive booklet spread like wildfire through the Western Hemisphere, and the Rider Waite Smith tarot deck established itself as the go-to deck for tarot readers, collectors, and enthusiasts.

U.S. Games has held the copyright and printing rights to the Rider Waite Smith tarot deck since 1971. They are the exclusive printer of these decks, which are a recreation, as the original printing plates were lost in a fire during WWII. Many modern decks vary from the RWS deck but all pay homage to the original through art and/or interpretation.

That's another thing about the Rider Waite Smith deck- not only did the art create a modern standard for tarot cards, but the RWS system also gave the world a widely-accepted interpretive guide. Combining the works of all who came before, including Court, Etteilla, Mathers, and Crowley, the interpretations written by Waite didn't take long to become the fundamental basis of interpretations used throughout the world. While interpretation is always an intuitive art, the cartomancy definitions written by Waite remain the most popular in use even into the 21st century.

The Use of Tarot Cards Today

Tarot has lasted since the 1400s, so who is still using it? The answer is lots of people! While there are some who scoff at tarot for divination as a parlor trick, there are just as many who hold a deep belief that a tarot deck can be a useful tool in guiding decision-making and 'seeing' the future. Some people offer tarot reading as a service provided by their spiritual health system or have incorporated it into a pagan or nature-centric religious lifestyle. Some people collect decks and interpretive guides for the artwork and take pride in finding and building unique decks. There is no wrong reason to collect, enjoy, read, and interpret tarot, as long as you keep in mind that the originators of tarot for divination did not intend for it to be used to inflict harm on others. We'll talk much more about the proper delivery of prophecy later in the book.

If you've decided that you want to read tarot, you probably have a compelling reason why, even if it's just innate curiosity. The best tarot readers are those that can immerse themselves in learning the history and the meanings of the cards, and use that knowledge combined with their intuition to be accurate and compassionate. Maybe you've been drawn to the cards because you are sensitive or empathic, and you want to explore ways to use that gift to help others. No matter your impetus behind wanting to learn tarot, you've come to the right place to find meaning, advice, and important notes about modern tarot.

Now that you've got a good basic understanding of where tarot originated and how it has evolved through the centuries, it's time to talk about the cards themselves. We'll be using the Rider Waite Smith deck as our model. Even if you decide to move onto other decks or learn to create your own decks, the RWS interpretations will be the foundation of the majority of interpretive guides you may read. Let's head on over to Chapter 2 and get started.

PART II
Understanding and Finding Meaning In The Tarot Deck

You now know that a 'standard' tarot deck has 78 cards split into the Major and Minor Arcana. Before we get into interpretation and intuition, it's important that you have a good foundation of knowing what each card looks like and what individual meaning is assigned to it. We'll break this chapter down into the suits and cards of the Minor Arcana, and then finish up with the illustrated depictions that make up the Major Arcana. Let's get started!

The Minor Arcana

There are 14 cards in each suit of the Minor Arcana, numbered 1 (ace) through 10, with four face cards, the knave (page), knight, queen, and king. Some decks replace the knave and knight with a princess and prince, although this seems to be more of a regional variation. Each card is assigned a meaning that varies on how it is facing when it is dealt- upright or reversed, based on whether the top or bottom of the card is facing you. If the card is upright, the bottom will be nearer to you and it looks correct. If the card is reversed, it will appear to be upside-down to you, and the top will be closest to you. The interpretation of the cards also relies on what the tarot reading is focused on- love, work, finances, health, or spirituality. The Minor Arcana is used to explore the happenings of everyday life and encourage thoughtful decision-making and self-reflection.

Wands (Batons, Clubs, or Staves)

The suit of Wands, or batons, clubs, or staves as they are sometimes known, is the suit that developed closely related to the suit of clubs in a deck of modern playing cards. This suit is meant to point out areas that require self-assessment like spirituality, determination, emotional strength, creativity, and ambition. In decks that play to the four elements of nature, Wands is meant to be the fire component. Fire is a masculine, primal element that speaks to the harsher side of nature, but can also be a cleansing experience.

Ace of Wands

- Description: This card most commonly depicts a hand holding a flaming torch in front of a cloud.

- Upright meaning: a call for creativity

- Reverse meaning: a delay in a creative project

- Basic interpretations: The Ace of Wands is most commonly related to the beginning of a new work endeavor, romantic relationship, or major project.

Two of Wands

- Description: This card most commonly depicts a man or woman holding a globe with two staves or rods in the picture.

- Upright meaning: call to set goals or find new ambitions

- Reverse meaning: a fear of the unknown or a lack of planning

- Basic interpretations: The Two of Wands is most commonly related to a world of new possibilities, including work prospects but the fear of leaving the comfort zone.

Three of Wands

- Description: This card most commonly depicts a figure with their back turned, surrounded by three staves or wands.

- Upright meaning: looking forward to opportunities, perhaps overseas

- Reverse meaning: delays, lack of planning, and oversights

- Basic interpretations: The Three of Wands is most commonly related to committing to new ideas and opportunities, and to taking a leap of faith.

Four of Wands

- Description: This card most commonly depicts four wands planted in the ground with garlands strung between them, and two people in celebration under the garland.

- Upright meaning: a homecoming celebration full of joy

- Reverse meaning: personal satisfaction that may be tainted with outer conflict

- Basic interpretations: The Four of Wands is most commonly related to people enjoying a personal milestone or accomplishment, or a sense of home.

Five of Wands

- Description: This card most commonly depicts five hands holding five wands, crossed as if fighting each other off.

- Upright meaning: showing tension, conflict, diversity

- Reverse meaning: related to inner conflict and turmoil

- Basic interpretations: The Five of Wands is most commonly related to people who cannot overcome differences, despite all factions being nearly the same.

Six of Wands

- Description: This card most commonly depicts a figure riding a horse, holding a wand, while others carry five wands around him/her.

- Upright meaning: progress, public recognition, self-confidence

- Reverse meaning: egotism, a fall from favor, personal satisfaction

- Basic interpretations: The Six of Wands is a card related to successes, both public and private, and how a person feels about those successes.

Seven of Wands

- Description: This card most commonly depicts a figure atop a hill, wearing two different shoes, with a stave pointing down towards six staves facing back at them.

- Upright meaning: perseverance, competition, challenge, and protection

- Reverse meaning: related to exhaustion, feeling overwhelmed

- Basic interpretations: The Seven of Wands is related to conflict and conflict resolution, as well as protecting one's territory under stress.

Eight of Wands

- Description: This card most commonly depicts a set of eight wands soaring through the air like arrows, sometimes accompanied by one or two birds.

- Upright meaning: forward movement, progress toward a goal, fast-paced action

- Reverse meaning: resistance to change, delays in reaching a destination

- Basic interpretations: The Eight of Wands is related to travel, personal growth, and progress, and dealing with setbacks that may cause major impediments.

Nine of Wands

- Description: This card most commonly depicts an injured figure, holding a staff in his uninjured hand while eight more wands or staff loom over their shoulder.

- Upright meaning: testing faith, boundaries, perseverance, courage, and resilience

- Reverse meaning: defensiveness, paranoia, struggles to overcome inner conflict

- Basic interpretations: The Nine of Wands is related to coming to the finish line of a struggle or conflict, both inner and outer.

Ten of Wands

- Description: This card most commonly depicts a figure carrying a bundle of ten wands on their bent back.

- Upright meaning: extra work, carrying a burden, nearing completion

- Reverse meaning: the stress of doing it all and carrying the whole load

- Basic interpretations: The Ten of Wands is related to people who have had a long road with a heavy pack and are nearing the end of their journey or struggle.

Knave of Wands

- Description: This card most commonly depicts a young man carrying a wand, which is acting as a torch, and his clothes are often adorned with salamanders, the animal fire spirit.

- Upright meaning: endless potential, new ideas and concepts, discovery

- Reverse meaning: limiting beliefs, new paths to spirituality

- Basic interpretations: The Knave of Wands is related to finding new opportunities waiting after a long period of conflict or burden.

Knight of Wands

- Description: This card most commonly depicts an armored knight upon a rearing steed. The knight carries a flaming staff, ready for battle, against a barren desert landscape, common to the Wands face cards.

- Upright meaning: energy, impulsiveness, readiness for action and adventure

- Reverse meaning: unfocused energy, delays in projects, haste

- Basic interpretations: The Knight of Wands is related to bursting with new energy and not being able to focus completely on the task or rushing to complete it.

Queen of Wands

- Description: This card most commonly depicts a queen sitting on a throne of lions with flowers surrounding her and a cat at her feet.

- Upright meaning: socialization, confidence, courage, independence

- Reverse meaning: introversion, self-reinvention, self-respect

- Basic interpretations: The Queen of Wands is related to finding satisfaction and joy within oneself and with other people through strong relationships and self-esteem.

Kings of Wands

- Description: This card most commonly depicts a king sitting on a throne, wearing a robe with salamanders and lions, and holding a single blooming wand.

- Upright meaning: honor, the entrepreneurial spirit, leadership

- Reverse meaning: impulsiveness, impossible expectations, haste

- Basic interpretations: The King of Wands is related to finding one's path to strong leadership, eschewing shortcuts, and overcoming obstacles.

Pentacles (Coins, Disks, or Rings)

Pentacles is the suit of the merchants and relates to the standard suit of diamonds. Pentacles, or as they are sometimes known, coins, disks, or rings, represent material possessions and matters of finance. This suit is associated with the element of earth because it deals with tangible objects. It is also considered to be a feminine element, dealing in the subtleties of business and relationships.

Ace of Pentacles

- Description: This card most commonly depicts a hand emerging from a cloud holding a large coin, against a backdrop of lush foliage and flowers.

- Upright meaning: abundance, a manifestation of wealth and opportunity

- Reverse meaning: lost opportunities, lack of planning

- Basic interpretations: The Ace of Pentacles is related to recognizing and seizing new business and opportunities when they are offered.

Two of Pentacles

- Description: This card most commonly depicts a man trying to juggle two coins connected by an infinity symbol. In the background, ships bob on an uncertain sea.

- Upright meaning: time management, priorities, and adaptability

- Reverse meaning: being disorganized, taking on too much responsibility

- Basic interpretations: The Two of Pentacles is related to being able to take on responsibility, so long as one is organized and sets good priorities.

Three of Pentacles

- Description: This card most commonly depicts three figures, a stonemason working while two others hold the plans. Three coins are suspended over their heads.

- Upright meaning: teamwork, progress, and collaboration

- Reverse meaning: being out of alignment, working alone, miscommunication

- Basic interpretations: The Three of Pentacles is related to being able to work as part of a team for the advancement of all parties, and the negative consequences of not doing so.

Four of Pentacles

- Description: This card most commonly depicts a figure hoarding four coins, holding one, one above their head, and two tucked between their feet.

- Upright meaning: control, financial security, and saving money

- Reverse meaning: greed and overspending

- Basic interpretations: The Four of Pentacles is related to the need to hold onto money, sometimes to the detriment of the holder.

Five of Pentacles

- Description: This card most commonly depicts a pair of figures who are evidently destitute, walking through cold weather with little protection as five coins float above their heads on a church window.

- Upright meaning: poverty, significant financial loss, isolation, and worry

- Reverse meaning: the recovery from financial hardship and lack of faith

- Basic interpretations: The Five of Pentacles is related to being in poverty, but being unable to see that help is available, symbolized in the coins on the church window as the poor figures trudge by without looking up.

Six of Pentacles

- Description: This card most commonly depicts a man in a rich red robe, holding a set of scales and distributing coins to two other figures.

- Upright meaning: generosity, sharing the wealth, and giving and receiving

- Reverse meaning: one-sided charity, unpaid debt

- Basic interpretations: The Six of Pentacles is related to being able to find the balance between personal wealth, taking care of oneself, and still being able to give to others.

Seven of Pentacles

- Description: This card most commonly depicts a garden that is growing on stems made of seven pentacles, the flowers of which are being tended by a figure holding a hoe or rake.

- Upright meaning: sustainability, perseverance, and long-term growth

- Reverse meaning: limited success, lack of vision

- Basic interpretations: The Seven of Pentacles is related to the ability to nurture an idea, relationship, or business dealing from start to finish and create a self-sustaining long-term solution to maintain that relationship.

Eight of Pentacles

- Description: This card most commonly depicts a man chiseling out the eight coins that surround him as he works outside of a city.

- Upright meaning: practice makes perfect, apprenticeship becoming mastery

- Reverse meaning: misguided energies, development, and perfectionism

- Basic interpretations: The Eight of Pentacles relates to mastery of a new skill or craft, sometimes to the exclusion of all other responsibilities and people.

Nine of Pentacles

- Description: This card most commonly depicts a woman in rich robes, surrounded by grapevines laden with coins and accompanied by a falcon.

- Upright meaning: financial independence, luxury, self-indulgence

- Reverse meaning: self-worth, overworking, hustling

- Basic interpretations: The Nine of Pentacles is related to being in control of one's wealth and taking the time to enjoy it, but also to wonder at what cost the wealth has come.

Ten of Pentacles

- Description: This card most commonly depicts an old man with his younger family and his dogs, seemingly spending time with them before he passes away, and they receive his wealth.

- Upright meaning: long-term family financial security, contribution to society

- Reverse meaning: financial loss, greed, the downside of wealth

- Basic interpretations: The Ten of Pentacles is related to how families are connected through inherited wealth and property, but also through an impact on each other and the community.

Knave of Pentacles

- Description: This card most commonly depicts a young man seemingly happy in a field of wheat or flowers. In the background, a mountain signifies both the opportunities and the challenges ahead.

- Upright meaning: skill development, the manifestation of hard work in wealth

- Reverse meaning: procrastination, self-indulgence, learning from failure

- Basic interpretations: The Knave of Pentacles is related to recognizing that wealth is not the end of the journey, and should be appreciated for a while but that it isn't the final goal.

Knight of Pentacles

- Description: This card most commonly depicts an armored knight seated upon a draft horse. He holds a golden pentacle in his hand and appears to be stationary.

- Upright meaning: conservative routines, self-assuredness, productivity

- Reverse meaning: boredom, self-discipline, being in a rut, perfectionism

- Basic interpretations: The Knight of Pentacles is related to being strong in one's convictions and certain in one's wealth and status.

Queen of Pentacles

- Description: This card most commonly depicts a queen sitting on a lush throne. She is cradling a golden coin and is accompanied by a rabbit, symbolizing fertility.

- Upright meaning: a working parent, nurturing, security, and wealth

- Reverse meaning: a conflict between work and home, financial independence

- Basic interpretations: The Queen of Pentacles is related to being financially secure enough that one feels nurturing of one's money as if it were a child to be protected.

King of Pentacles

- Description: This card most commonly depicts a king upon a throne, surrounded by gold, grapes, and other signs of abundance.

- Upright meaning: wealth and power, security, and leadership

- Reverse meaning: an obsession with status, financial illiteracy, stubbornness

- Basic interpretations: The King of Pentacles is related to creating wealth and financial security, and wanting to show off that abundance to others.

Cups (Chalices)

The suit of Cups is related to the hearts suit in standard playing cards. This suit is used to discern what is happening and will happen in matters of love, relationships, and emotional events. Its elemental facet is that of water and is usually characterized as feminine because it deals with emotions, love, and intuition.

Ace of Cups

- Description: This card is most commonly depicted as a chalice that is overflowing. The water comes down in five streams to represent the five senses, and a hand, emerging from clouds like the other aces, attempts to catch the overflowing liquid.

- Upright meaning: new relationships, new love, and compassion

- Reverse meaning: intuition, self-love, and repression of emotions

- Basic interpretations: The Ace of Cups is related to the mixture of emotions experienced when forming new romantic or interpersonal relationships, and the self-reflection and intuition needed to do so.

Two of Cups

- Description: This card most commonly depicts a pair of young lovers, sharing a cup holding a caduceus (intertwined snakes) topped with a lion's head.

- Upright meaning: partnership, mutual attraction, and unification

- Reverse meaning: disharmony and distrust, the breakup of relationships

- Basic interpretations: The Two of Cups is related to the commencement of partnerships, romantic entanglements, and commerce.

Three of Cups

- Description: This card most commonly depicts three women dancing in a circle. They are holding their cups up in a salute or toast of celebration.

- Upright meaning: the joy of companionship, collaboration, and creativity

- Reverse meaning: independence, partying to excess, being a 'third wheel'

- Basic interpretations: The Three of Cups is related to matters of young friendship, including both the joy and the social discord that can come from these types of relationships.

Four of Cups

- Description: This card most commonly depicts a figure sitting under a tree as if in meditation. There are three cups before them and a hand offering a fourth, but the person seems oblivious to what's right in front of them.

- Upright meaning: Apathy, reevaluation, meditation, and reflection

- Reverse meaning: Withdrawal or retreat from the outside world

- Basic interpretations: The Four of Cups is related to self-reflection and observation and whether it is better to live within one's one head or participate more in the outside world.

Five of Cups

- Description: This card most commonly depicts a cloaked figure with their back turned. They are looking at the ground at three spilled cups, while two intact cups sit to their other side.

- Upright meaning: Disappointment, pessimism, failure, and regret

- Reverse meaning: Setbacks, moving forward from failure, self-forgiveness

- Basic interpretations: The Five of Cups is related to being able to recognize mistakes and move on, and being able to see new possibilities even though one has suffered a perceived failure.

Six of Cups

- Description: This card most commonly depicts a pair of children with six cups of flowers. Five of the cups rest on the ground as one child hands the other the sixth cup.

- Upright meaning: revisiting childhood memories, nostalgia, and innocence

- Reverse meaning: lack of joy, living in the past, finding forgiveness

- Basic interpretations: The Six of Cups is related to finding joy and security in childhood memories, and finding love and harmony in lifelong relationships.

Seven of Cups

- Description: This card most commonly depicts a figure standing in front of six chalices, each of which has a different object or gift in it.

- Upright meaning: wishful thinking, dreams, and aspirations

- Reverse meaning: being overwhelmed by choices, defining personal values

- Basic interpretations: The Seven of Cups is related to making decisions regarding the future. The various gifts in the chalices are symbolic of the paths that life can take, depending on what one chooses.

Eight of Cups

- Description: This card most commonly depicts a figure walking away into the mountains, while eight cups sit in the foreground.

- Upright meaning: withdrawal, escapism, disappointment, and abandonment

- Reverse meaning: indecision, walking away from failure, aimlessness

- Basic interpretations: The Eight of Cups is related to a lack of personal or emotional fulfillment, or the need to cut losses and walk away from disappointments.

Nine of Cups

- Description: This card most commonly depicts a figure with their arms crossed, sitting on a bench with an arch of nine cups above their head. The figure is smiling with satisfaction.

- Upright meaning: contentment, dreams come true, satisfaction

- Reverse meaning: materialism and indulgence, smugness

- Basic interpretations: The Nine of Cups is related to feeling content after an accomplishment or personal satisfaction in relationships or wealth levels.

Ten of Cups

- Description: This card most commonly depicts a young family with their backs turned, looking at their home. Above them, ten cups are stretched in an arch as if they are a rainbow through the sky.

- Upright meaning: harmony, alignment with family, divine love

- Reverse meaning: relationship struggles, misalignment of goals

- Basic interpretations: The Ten of Cups is related to finding family harmony and success by working towards mutual goals.

Knave of Cups

- Description: This card most commonly depicts the knave wearing a flowing robe against a backdrop of the ocean or sea. In their hand is a cup containing a fish.

- Upright meaning: curiosity, new opportunities, intuition, and creativity

- Reverse meaning: emotional or creative blocks, immaturity

- Basic interpretations: The Knave of Cups is related to the flow of creativity and the finding of unexpected inspiration and opportunities.

Knight of Cups

- Description: This card most commonly depicts a knight on a white horse, wearing a winged hat and boots and a robe adorned with fish. The knight carries a golden cup near to his heart.

- Upright meaning: romance, beauty, charm, and imagination

- Reverse meaning: jealousy, unrealistic expectations, overactive imagination

- Basic interpretations: The Knight of Cups is related to finding love and beauty without having unrealistic expectations of others. It also carries the symbolism of peace and power, as the knight is not charging into battle, but serenely riding his horse forward into the future.

Queen of Cups

- Description: This card most commonly depicts a queen holding a golden chalice, observing the ocean from a golden throne. An arc over her cup shows that nothing may enter or escape the chalice.

- Upright meaning: emotional stability, intuition in love and life

- Reverse meaning: codependency, self-love, and self-care

- Basic interpretations: The Queen of Cups is related to self-reflection, finding emotional stability, and the ability to be self-reliant and self-loving.

King of Cups

- Description: This card most commonly depicts a king upon a golden seaside throne. He holds a golden cup, wears a fish on a pendant over his robes, and is observing the boats upon the water.

- Upright meaning: compassion, emotional balance

- Reverse meaning: moodiness and manipulation, inner feelings

- Basic interpretations: The King of Cups is related to staying calm and finding balance even amongst inner turmoil. The calm he shows as boats are rocked on the waves is symbolic of riding out an emotional storm with power and grace.

Swords (Spades)

The suit of Swords, or sometimes spades, equates to the playing card suit of spades, and this is the suit of the military and nobility. It is used to read concerns about reasoning and conflict and relies heavily on the imagery of the sword having a double-edge. The Swords are the air elemental suit. This traditionally masculine suit and element rely heavily on the imagery of wind to show change and movement.

Ace of Swords

- Description: This card most commonly depicts a single sword being held upright by a hand emerging from a white cloud (as is common with all the other aces). A mountain rises jagged in the background.

- Upright meaning: mental clarity, new ideas, brainstorming

- Reverse meaning: rethinking concepts, clouded decision-making

- Basic interpretations: The Ace of Swords is related to being able to make clear-cut decisions and being willing to do the follow-up work to make those decisions come to fruition.

Two of Swords

- Description: This card most commonly depicts a robed, blind-folded figure, arms crossed with a sword in each hand, pointing upward. The figure is often standing in front of a rocky coastline.

- Upright meaning: weighing choices, making difficult decisions

- Reverse meaning: confusion, feeling overwhelmed, indecision

- Basic interpretations: The Two of Swords is related to the difficulties of decision making when one feels confused or like they don't have all the necessary information to make a good choice.

Three of Swords

- Description: This card most commonly depicts a large heart being pierced by three downward-facing swords, on a background of dark clouds.

- Upright meaning: grief, heartbreak, sorrow, and emotional pain

- Reverse meaning: optimism, forgiveness, letting go, negative self-talk

- Basic interpretations: The Three of Swords is related to grief at the end of personal relationships and finding the strength to let go and move forward without permanent emotional damage.

Four of Swords

- Description: This card most commonly depicts a scene of a knight laid to rest with his sword, as three more swords hang above him. There is often a woman and child shown in the background.

- Upright meaning: rest, contemplation, relaxation, and meditation

- Reverse meaning: burn-out, overwhelming stress, stagnation, and exhaustion

- Basic interpretations: The Four of Swords is related to finding a balance between singular focus and being able to relax and recuperate. The sword with the knight symbolizes his ambition, while his pose suggests he may have lost his life as a result.

Five of Swords

- Description: This card most commonly depicts a figure in the foreground holding a sword, while two figures in the background sadly look over a battlefield strewn with four other swords.

- Upright meaning: defeat, competition, victory at all costs, conflict

- Reverse meaning: making amends, putting aside past resentments, burying the hatchet

- Basic interpretations: The Five of Swords is related to conflict and conflict resolution, and being able to move on even though there may be fresh feelings of hurt or sadness.

Six of Swords

- Description: This card most commonly depicts a woman holding a child close to her as they ride in a small boat. Six swords are arranged in the boat, suggesting that they are being protected and moved away from an area of conflict. The sea behind them is raging while the sea before them is calm.

- Upright meaning: rites of passage, times of transition

- Reverse meaning: personal growth and change, unfinished business

- Basic interpretations: The Six of Swords is related to finding peace after experiencing turmoil and being able to move away from conflict and find peace, no matter what that takes.

Seven of Swords

- Description: This card most commonly depicts a man sneaking away from a military encampment, carrying five swords. He is looking both smug about his theft and worried that he left two swords behind.

- Upright meaning: betrayal and deception, creating strategies

- Reverse meaning: self-deceit, imposter syndrome, secret-keeping

- Basic interpretations: The Seven of Swords is related to being covert and strategic, and creating deception of self and others.

Eight of Swords

- Description: This card most commonly depicts a figure who is standing near water and is bound and blindfolded, surrounded by eight upright swords.

- Upright meaning: imprisonment, self-limiting, negative thoughts

- Reverse meaning: releasing negativity, being an inner critic

- Basic interpretations: The Eight of Swords is related to being stuck in a victim mentality, limiting oneself with negative self-talk and criticism, and being able to remove the ties that bind to find freedom.

Nine of Swords

- Description: This card most commonly depicts a woman who is sitting upright in bed, covering her face with her hands. It's to be understood that she may have suffered a nightmare. Nine swords hang on the wall in her bed-chamber.

- Upright meaning: anxiety, fear, depression, nightmares, and worries

- Reverse meaning: deep-seated anxieties and fears, releasing stress and worry

- Basic interpretations: The Nine of Swords is related to fear and anxiety that is often rooted deep in the psyche and manifests itself during sleep.

Ten of Swords

- Description: This card depicts a figure lying face down with ten swords in their back. The sun is setting in the distant background as the body is shown to be dead or dying.

- Upright meaning: betrayal, deep emotional wounds, loss, and crisis

- Reverse meaning: regeneration and recovery

- Basic interpretations: The Ten of Swords is related to finding solace and moving on even after the darkest hours, showing that death (literal or figurative) is not necessarily the end.

Knave of Swords

- Description: This card most commonly depicts a young knave holding his sword upright but looking the in the opposite direction from the side where he is carrying his blade as if to assess his surroundings. Clouds are moving behind him, and he is standing in a green field.

- Upright meaning: curiosity, new ideas, seeking new knowledge

- Reverse meaning: haste, wasted actions, all talk, no results

- Basic interpretations: The Knave of Swords is related to being curious about the world but often being ignorant or naïve about what is really going on, leading to miscues and wasted energy.

Knight of Swords

- Description: This card most commonly depicts a knight, sword held aloft, charging forward on a winged horse. Storm clouds are gathering behind him as he surges toward a battle.

- Upright meaning: thinking on one's feet, ambition, success-driven

- Reverse meaning: impulsive, restless, headed toward burn-out

- Basic interpretations: The Knight of Swords is related to being so ambitious that one can think and act quickly, often suffering the drawbacks of being too impulsive.

Queen of Swords

- Description: This card most commonly depicts a queen on a low throne, surrounded by butterflies. She holds a sword in her right hand and is looking ahead while storm clouds gather behind her.

- Upright meaning: independence, direct communication, clear judgment

- Reverse meaning: cold-hearted, emotional, easy to influence

- Basic interpretations: The Queen of Swords is related to being able to make transformative decisions with good judgment, despite the connotation of being emotionally hard or being called unstable.

King of Swords

- Description: This card is commonly depicted very similarly to its queen, with a king sitting on a low throne, sword in his right hand, left hand with the palm open facing skyward. A storm clouds behind the king seem to settle down as he fixes his gaze straight ahead.

- Upright meaning: intellectual truths and power, mental strength

- Reverse meaning: abuse of power, manipulation

- Basic interpretations: The King of Swords is related to being able to find strength and clarity after a period of turmoil, and retain the power of intellectual truth over one's opponents.

Now that you've got a guide to the cards of the Minor Arcana and what their individual meanings are, let's take a look at the Major Arcana and what these cards look like and their basic interpretations.

The Major Arcana

The Major Arcana is made up of the 22 trump cards of a tarot deck. These cards are all picture cards, depicting scenes that are interpreted based upon the allegory shown and the order in which the cards are dealt. The Major Arcana is used to determine the status and impending happenings of important life events, to be used for decision-making and spiritual reflection.

The Fool

- Description: The Fool is the only unnumbered card in the Major Arcana. He is often the 'main' character in the tarot journey. The Fool card most commonly shows a man departing on a trip, walking near the precipice of a cliff, carrying a small pack or knapsack. He is often holding a rose and may or may not be accompanied by a companion animal like a small dog. The card may sometimes be displayed with a zero instead of a lack of a number.

- Upright meaning: New beginnings, being spontaneous, the spirit of adventure

- Reverse meaning: recklessness, senseless risk-taking

- Basic interpretations: The Fool is related to undertaking a new adventure of any kind, and serves as a reminder to be brave enough to try, but smart enough to know there may be great challenges ahead.

The Magician

- Description: The Magician is the #1 card in the Major Arcana. This card most commonly depicts a robed figure, standing under an infinity sign, holding aloft a staff. On the table in front of him are a cup, sword, pentacle, and wand, symbolizing the unity of the four suits of the Minor Arcana.

- Upright meaning: being resourceful, taking positive, decisive action

- Reverse meaning: manipulation, untapped potential, lack of planning

- Basic interpretations: The Magician is related to recognizing and striving to meet potential and not leaving opportunities to go to waste. The Magician's hands are pointing both skyward and to the ground, symbolizing the need to reach high but remain realistic.

The High Priestess

- Description: The High Priestess is the #2 card in the Major Arcana. This card most commonly depicts a woman holding a globe, with celestial bodies adorning her robe. She is standing between the pillars at the entrance to her temple, looking serenely to one side.

- Upright meaning: feminism, intuition, divine knowledge, and the subconscious

- Reverse meaning: withdrawal, silence, poor intuition

- Basic interpretations: The High Priestess is related to divine feminism, the secrets of intuition and the sacred, and the ability to use that intuition for the greater good. The High Priestess gives the impression of knowing what not many others know, but that she may be willing to impart that knowledge if you follow her ways.

The Empress

- Description: The Empress is the #3 card in the Major Arcana. This card most commonly depicts a young woman seated upon a pile of lush cushions, holding a pomegranate or other fruit, and surrounded by nature. She wears a crown of twelve stars and is shown as the symbolism of fertility.

- Upright meaning: abundant nature, beauty, nature

- Reverse meaning: dependency on others, creative setbacks or blocks

- Basic interpretations: The Empress is related to being in tune with nature and letting the harmony of the natural world help someone align their own desires and needs.

The Emperor

- Description: The Emperor is the #4 card in the Major Arcana. This card most commonly depicts an older man seated on a grand throne. He is holding an orb to signify his power over the world, and in his other hand is a wand. The throne may be decorated with animal skulls to show his power in the natural world as well.

- Upright meaning: the establishment of the patriarchy, authority

- Reverse meaning: domination, inflexibility, controlling, stubborn

- Basic interpretations: The Emperor is related to power and authority that doesn't allow for shows of emotion. The mountains and river depicted in the background of this card show that it's okay to let emotions flow even past a rocky exterior.

The Pope

- Description: The Pope is the #5 card in the Major Arcana, sometimes also known as the Teacher or the Hierophant. This card most commonly depicts a religious figure between the pillars at the head of a temple. He is holding a staff, often with crossbars, and wears a belt of crossed keys.

- Upright meaning: traditions and conformity, divine knowledge

- Reverse meaning: freedom, challenge norms, personal beliefs

- Basic interpretations: The Pope is related to finding and understanding personal and religious truths. The card symbolizes the relationship between the earth and the divine and the keepers of that relationship.

The Lovers

- Description: The Lovers is the #6 card in the Major Arcana. This card most commonly depicts a naked couple under the watchful eye of the archangel Raphael, who is there to remind them of their love for each other as well as for the divine.

- Upright meaning: unity, harmony, love in personal relationships

- Reverse meaning: misalignment, disharmony, romantic tensions

- Basic interpretations: The Lovers is related to finding common ground in personal relationships. The background of the card, which shows a garden (perhaps Eden), symbolizes the need to work together to achieve common goals and overcome hardships together.

The Chariot

- Description: The Chariot is the #7 card in the Major Arcana. This card most commonly depicts a warrior in a chariot, whose armor is adorned with a crescent moon and other alchemic symbols. The chariot is pulled by a pair of sphinxes, and he has a field of six stars above his head.

- Upright meaning: willpower, determination, action, and control

- Reverse meaning: lack of direction, opposition, self-discipline

- Basic interpretations: The Chariot is related to taking action, forging new paths forward, and connecting to the unknown to create new successes. The charioteer's tall posture is symbolic of being determined and not fearing the unknown.

Strength

- Description: Strength is the #8 card in the Major Arcana. This card most commonly depicts a woman in a shimmering robe with a lion, whose head she is stroking. She wears a belt of flowers and an infinity symbol in her hair.

- Upright meaning: Courage, persuasion, influence, and compassion

- Reverse meaning: self-doubt, hidden emotions, inner strength, and lack of energy

- Basic interpretations: Strength is related to situations that call for resilience, powers of persuasion, and positive inner strength. The lion is tame, symbolizing the woman's ability to take even the wildest of beasts in stride.

The Hermit

- Description: The Hermit is the #9 card in the Major Arcana. This card most commonly depicts an old man standing alone atop a mountain, holding a lantern. The man is also using a walking stick and wearing full-length robes.

- Upright meaning: introspection, being alone, seeking inner guidance

- Reverse meaning: loneliness, withdrawal

- Basic interpretations: The Hermit is related to the need for self-reflection to produce personal growth. His lantern lets off a six-pointed star of light, symbolizing the wisdom of Solomon, widely regarded as the sagest of the biblical patriarchs.

The Wheel of Fortune

- Description: The Wheel of Fortune is the #10 card in the Major Arcana. This card most commonly depicts a large wheel, divided into eight segments. The letters TORA are placed at the cardinal points of the wheel, meaning the Torah, an almost-anagram for tarot, or 'rota,' the Latin word for wheel, and the elemental symbols for earth, air, water, and fire within the wheel. There are mythical creatures placed around the perimeter of the card, and the wheel features an arrow that would function as a spinner.

- Upright meaning: luck, life cycles, good karma, a turning point

- Reverse meaning: resistance to change, breaking cycles, bad luck

- Basic interpretations: The Wheel of Fortune relates to matters of luck, both good and bad. It also can represent the need to complete or break a cycle in one's life.

Justice

- Description: Justice is the #11 card in the Major Arcana. The card most commonly depicts a woman, presumed to be Lady Justice, in a long purple robe, carrying a sword and scales. She wears a crown and stands between two pillars, similar to the High Priestess and the Pope.

- Upright meaning: truth, justice, balance, and good judgment

- Reverse meaning: dishonesty, lack of accountability

- Basic interpretations: Justice is related to matters that require fair judgment and personal responsibility. She symbolizes the need to remember that truth is a double-edged sword and that people will be judged by others, but also need to be true to themselves.

The Hanged Man

- Description: The Hanged Man is the #12 card in the Major Arcana. This card most commonly depicts a man hanged from his ankles on either a cross or a live tree. His hands are also bound behind his back, and he's often shown with a halo.

- Upright meaning: surrender, pausing for reflection, finding new perspectives

- Reverse meaning: indecision, stalling for time, delays, and resistance

- Basic interpretations: The Hanged Man is related to situations that need further thought before making major decisions. His serenity shows that he is not in pain, but instead, is quietly reflecting on the path that led to his current predicament.

Death

- Description: Death is the #13 card in the Major Arcana. This card most commonly depicts a skeleton in black armor riding a white horse along a seashore. He carries a flag and wears keys at his waist. Boats bob on the water behind him as a woman lays herself down at his horse's feet, imploring him to spare her dead loved one.

- Upright meaning: change, endings, transitions

- Reverse meaning: personal growth and transformation, resisting change

- Basic interpretations: Death is related to the natural end of all things. This card is regarded as one of the most important because it can symbolize the need for someone to make life-changing decisions before they are made for them.

Temperance

- Description: Temperance is the #14 card in the Major Arcana. This card most commonly depicts a large androgynous angel who is hovering over the ground carrying a large urn or two drinking chalices. The angel is in front of a harsh desert or mountain landscape and is transferring liquid from a cup to the urn or between the two cups.

- Upright meaning: moderation, patience, balance, and purpose

- Reverse meaning: excess, imbalance, loss of purpose or direction

- Basic interpretations: Temperance is related to the need to keep a balance in life, not to do anything to excess, and to have patience and moderation in all things.

The Devil

- Description: The Devil is the #15 card in the Major Arcana. This card most commonly depicts a large horned goat, to symbolize Baphomet. A man and a woman are being enslaved by the horned goat figure, and their shackles are being held to the Devil's chair. The shackles are loose enough that the pair could escape, but you can see that they are beginning to also sprout horns. This indicates that the longer one stays in the presence of evil, the more one becomes evil themselves.

- Upright meaning: addiction, self-deceit, sexuality, restriction of freedoms

- Reverse meaning: the exploration of dark beliefs, shadows, self-doubt

- Basic interpretations: The Devil is related to the darker side of life, magick, and the occult. The card is often interpreted as a warning to be mindful of getting involved with things one doesn't understand or may not be able to get away from once the decision is made.

The Tower

- Description: The Tower is the #16 card in the Major Arcana. This card most commonly depicts a scene of death and destruction, as the large mountain top tower is struck by lightning and set afire. Figures can be seen leaping from the window of the tower to their ultimate fate.

- Upright meaning: upheaval, sudden changes, chaos, and awakening

- Reverse meaning: fear of change, being able to avert disaster, transformation

- Basic interpretations: The Tower is related to any unexpected upheavals, any crumbling of goals and relationships founded upon false pretenses, or stress that comes in and causes fear and disruption.

The Star

- Description: The Star is the #17 card in the Major Arcana. This card most commonly depicts a naked woman kneeling beside a pond, with one foot in the water and her other knee on land. She is filling two bowls, one which she dumps upon the ground to nourish the earth. It comes out in five streams to symbolize the five senses. She often has a crown of stars in her hair to signify an additional connection to the cosmos.

- Upright meaning: hope, renewal, fertility, purpose, and spirituality

- Reverse meaning: lack of faith, despair, miscommunication

- Basic interpretations: The Star is related to using both spirituality and practicality to find one's way to new beginnings.

The Moon

- Description: The Moon is the #18 card in the Major Arcana. This card most commonly depicts the moon hanging large in the sky between two towers. A dog and a wolf, symbolizing both the tame and the wild, howl at the moon. There is often also a small pool of water on this card, and a lobster or crawfish may be depicted leaving the pool.

- Upright meaning: intuition, the subconscious, fear, anxiety, and illusion

- Reverse meaning: the release of worry and fear, confusion, and repressed emotions

- Basic interpretations: The Moon is related to matters concerning following one's head or one's heart. The main takeaway from this card is that the subconscious will guide someone into behaviors they may not willingly want to do- just as the tame dog howls at the moon alongside his wild counterpart.

The Sun

- Description: The Sun is the #19 card in the Major Arcana. This card most commonly depicts a young child riding a white horse under a blazing sky. The child is carrying a staff, and the horse is adorned with flowers.

- Upright meaning: fun, possibility, warmth, success, vitality

- Reverse meaning: being overly optimistic, feeling down, exposing the inner child

- Basic interpretations: The Sun is related to the need for optimism and the opportunity to find success. The card suggests that being able to connect with one's inner child may be the impetus needed to find joy in new things and appreciate what one already has.

Judgment

- Description: Judgment is the #20 card in the Major Arcana. This card most commonly depicts people- men, women, and children- rising from the grave and rising toward a sky dominated by the heraldic appearance of the archangel Gabriel.

- Upright meaning: rebirth, renewal, finding a new calling

- Reverse meaning: self-doubt, ignoring opportunity, missing one's calling

- Basic interpretations: Judgement is related to taking advantage of new chances and putting one's old life behind them. This card is often interpreted to be a sign that it's time to make a major life decision or stop second-guessing oneself.

The World

- Description: The World is the #21 card in the Major Arcana. This card most commonly depicts a woman dancing inside a large laurel wreath. She is wearing an infinity symbol in her hair, is carrying a wand in each hand, and signifies the full circle of life and the human experience.

- Upright meaning: accomplishment, completion of a cycle, travel

- Reverse meaning: seeking closure, running into delays, taking short-cuts

- Basic interpretations: The World relates to finding one's path through thoughtful decision-making and finishing one's purpose before moving on to a new one. The symbols placed around the perimeter of the card remind one to honor the elements and oneself.

Because it's rare to only deal one tarot card, all of the meanings and individual interpretations that you learned about in this chapter need to be tied together to make sense. In the next part, we'll be talking about the different deals and layouts you can use for your tarot readings. We'll also discuss how the cards can be interpreted together based on the situation and your intuition to determine an accurate divination. It's going to be a lot of information, but it's also getting into the best part of tarot- the excitement of reading and interpretation. Ready to start? Let's go!

PART III
Dealing and Interpreting The Tarot Deck

Knowing the history of the tarot deck and the significance of each card is the foundation you need to get started on the next step, that of dealing and interpreting the tarot deck. This part will be split into two main sections packed with information, and this is where you'll start learning about the different layouts for dealing and the intricacies of reading the cards in each layout. The second half of this part will talk about using your intuition and people-reading skills to put together the most accurate readings for your subjects. We'll also touch upon reading the cards for yourself, although the majority of that topic will be addressed in Part IV when we talk about the applications of tarot in the modern world. Let's begin with layouts.

Basic Tarot Dealing and Reading

We're going to start with a few simple, minimal-card layouts to get you familiarized with basic readings; then, we'll add a few more cards and layouts before moving onto the advanced layouts. The most important thing to remember, before you begin, is that your belief in the cards will be reflected in the subject's belief in the cards. You should be completely transparent when you begin a reading. Shuffle the deck in front of the person whose reading you are performing. You can ask them to cut the cards, only if you are comfortable with that or if they would like to. Some people prefer not to touch an occult object, and some people like to cut the cards because it gives them a connection and a sense that they can have a direct effect on which cards are dealt.

The following layouts will have very few cards and are generally used to address a single issue or area of concern- a big decision that needs to be made, a problem in your subject's personal or work life, or something that is a source of frustration or upset. You can use these deals to help yourself, your friends and family, and even strangers just find a little clarity, a sense of direction, or a nudge towards self-reflection. When you perform these layouts, you can ask the subject to either verbalize their question to you or to close their eyes and concentrate their thoughts on the matter while you shuffle and deal, thereby directing their concerns and energies towards the deck.

Past-Present-Future

This deal is exactly what it sounds like. Shuffle the cards and deal three, left to right in front of you. The card on the left is the past, in the center is the present, and to the right is the future. The past card gives context on what has already occurred and can explain what has caused the lead-up to the present. The interpretation of the present card can explain what is going on right now that might have seemed vague or needed context to uncover something going on under the surface. The future card is not necessarily a set-in-stone prediction but is instead an indicator of what could happen or what the present course of action is pointing toward.

This layout is a great way to use tarot cards to supplement or guide critical thinking skills when a difficult decision needs to be made. It is simple, not open to wild interpretation, and can give someone peace of mind that they are traveling the right path or open their eyes to the need to put more thought into an important course of action.

Examples:

6 Pentacles (upright), The Empress (reversed), 10 Wands (upright): This deal shows that your subject was prone to generosity and acts of giving in the past, and that led to a present which includes a dependence on others. Perhaps they've come to rely on the praise for their generosity to fuel their ego or make them feel justified in their existence. The ten of wands as the future card in this deal indicates that the person could feel burdened and as if they are the only one who does all the work. This may indicate that the subject needs to examine their giving nature and dependency on the positive feedback from others before they start to feel resentful as though they are the only one doing anything for other people. This reading can help the subject make decisions about their motives in helping others and how that can amend their thinking or their actions to be more aligned with their true intent.

<u>5 wands (reversed), 9 pentacles (upright), 8 swords (upright)</u>: In this deal, we find the five of wands upside down in the past slot, which shows that the subject was dealing with a great deal of inner conflict or feeling challenged or attacked. The present card shows that they have gotten past that and achieved self-sufficiency and stability. The eight of swords in the future slot indicates a sense of restriction and negative thinking, meaning that the subject may not feel confident in their self-support and might think that being financially stable may not be as liberating as they'd hoped. This reading can show the subject that there are upsides and downsides to success and indicate that they may need to do some self-reflection to decide if financial success equals true happiness.

Blessings- Challenges- Actions

This three-card layout is useful for finding direction when faced with a difficult decision or troublesome situation. Like the last layout, it's as simple as shuffling and dealing three cards left to right. The first card on the left is the blessings card. It indicates something positive that will be of use to the subject during the decision-making process. The middle card is the challenges card, and it shows something that may present an obstacle or is the source of trouble. The third card on the right is the actions card, and this indicates what may need to be done to solve the issue or come to a solid conclusion.

Examples:

<u>7 swords (reversed), The Lovers (reversed), 9 cups (upright)</u>: The blessings card here may seem unhelpful, but since it can indicate secret-keeping, it is likely showing that discretion will be a necessary and useful skill during the decision-making process. The reversed lovers are a sign that a relationship is out of balance and that values are not in alignment. This is the source of the need for a solution, and there may be resistance to change by one of the partners. The actions card in the upright nine of cups, and this card signifies contentment and a wish come true. The subject of this reading will have to examine what it is that is causing an imbalance in their relationship and, using discretion (which in this day and age, could likely point to not airing dirty laundry on social media),

find a way to compromise and find contentment in the relationship.

<u>The Emperor (upright), 4 cups (upright), 8 pentacles (reversed)</u>: In this deal, the blessings card is the Emperor, which signifies authority or a father figure. This is an indication that the subject of the reading has someone important on their side who will support their decision. The challenges card here is the upright four of cups, and while this is normally a positive card, it can indicate a lack of seriousness or care. The subject should examine their own behavior to see if their nonchalance may be the root of their concern. The reversed eight of pentacles shows a path to self-reflection, perfectionism, and self-development. This reading could be a larger indication that the subject is on a dead-end path, but through self-examination and the support of a father figure, they can right the ship by learning to put more care and feeling into their behaviors and actions.

Situation- Action- Results

This is another three-card deal, and again, you will shuffle and deal the cards left to right. The left-hand card indicates the scenario that is causing concern or needs to be addressed. The center card shows the action that can be taken to find a resolution, and the right-hand card is one of the possible results. The subject can use this deal to determine what needs to be done to get a problematic issue from Point A to Point B with a satisfactory conclusion.

Examples:

<u>10 cups (reversed), 6 swords (upright), 5 pentacles (reversed)</u>: The situation indicated by the ten of cups in this deal involves unhappy relationships, and this can show a lack of harmony at work or in love. The upright six of swords shows that a transition is needed to come to a resolution. The reversed five of pentacles in the results slot shows a financial or spiritual recovery, and so the totality of this reading could indicate that the subject needs to examine the cause of their imbalanced relationship, find a way to transition back into harmony, and if all goes well, they will find healing and recovery on the other side.

<u>Knave pentacles (upright), 7 cups (reversed), 8 cups (reversed)</u>: This deal shows the knave of pentacles in the situation slot, which is a card that indicates the development and manifestation of skills and finding financial opportunities. The reversed action card of the seven of cups shows that there may be too many choices and the subject is feeling overwhelmed. As an action card, this would indicate that they must find a way to narrow down the options regarding those opportunities. The reversed eight of cups in the results slot shows indecision and walking away from an opportunity. This reading, when interpreted as a whole, may show the subject that some of their alleged opportunities may not be exactly what they seem and that they should give all options careful consideration before taking their chances or walking away.

No Spread Layout

This layout is a deal of three cards and is more of a freeform, story-telling reading. There is no assigned position or order to the cards that you draw; this layout is open to interpretation, and each card indicates another layer of the story they are meant to tell. Like the other basic layouts, you should shuffle the deck and deal three cards left to right. Perform the reading by interpreting the three cards individually and then use your intuition to 'collate' the full reading from what's in front of you.

Examples:

<u>9 swords (upright), King pentacles (upright), 4 cups (reversed)</u>: Here we see the nine of swords, which indicates anxiety and fear, the king of pentacles, which indicates abundance, wealth, and security, and the reversed four of cups, which shows the need for or action of retreat and withdrawal or the need to perform a self-alignment. These cards are not overwhelmingly positive, but they don't have to indicate something bad. The subject of the reading may be financially secure but may suffer from anxiety about losing that wealth. They may need to withdraw and perform some self-care to relax and assure themselves that they have nothing to worry about. An alternate interpretation might be that someone is on the cusp of becoming wealthy or secure, but their fear is holding them back from reaching that goal. Again, a retreat or withdrawal for

self-reflection may be needed to help ease the mind and solve the issue.

10 pentacles (reversed), The Chariot (upright), 2 swords (upright): In this deal, we are faced with the reversed ten of pentacles, which indicates a financial loss, the chariot, which shows success and determination, and the two of swords which indicates difficult decisions and the need to weigh options. This reading is easily interpreted for the subject as an indicator to be careful when making large financial decisions. The double-edged blade indicated by the two of swords shows that major financial choices all have pros and cons, and being willing to examine the options closely before making a decision could be the difference between success and failure.

Clarifying Card

Before we move on to larger, more complex deals and interpretations, it's important to note the potential use of a clarifying card. Three cards is a fairly small sample size to make a clear reading, and that's why these deals are usually focused on one specific problem or need that the subject would like addressed. If you find that something feels lacking, you may draw a fourth card in any of these layouts to seek clarification or tie the three cards together a little better. Try not to use this all the time- you don't want to feel like it's a crutch or necessary for your interpretations. You want to learn to trust the cards and your intuition to perform complete readings without needing to deal an extra.

Advanced Tarot Dealing and Reading

Dealing larger layouts and making more in-depth interpretations may seem a little nerve-wracking when you're getting your start in tarot reading. Practice makes as perfect as can be on these larger deals, and there will be plenty of examples to help you think critically about how you interpret the cards. Like with the smaller deals, it is helpful to know what the subject of the reading's intentions and expectations are before you begin the reading. This helps you know what areas you should focus on while interpreting the cards. We'll talk much more about managing expectations and how much information you should or shouldn't disclose in the second segment of this part of the book, so for now, let's look at the layouts, the proper order for reading, and some examples to give you an idea of how the cards interact.

Three-Column

The three-column layout is a larger extension of the past-present-future spread, in which you will lay out nine cards instead of three. This deal gives a larger context than the three-card spread, allowing for a more in-depth analysis of a problem or a decision that needs to be made. In a three-column deal, you will shuffle the cards and lay them out in sets of three- left, center, right, left, center, right, left, center, right- or starting at the left- top, middle, bottom, top middle, bottom, top, middle, bottom. The left column is the past, the center column represents the present, and the right-hand column shows the potential future.

Examples:

*The query: The subject is trying to decide whether to take a promotion at work, but it would require a major relocation.

Column 1- Ace pentacles (upright), 6 cups (reversed), 10 wands (upright)

Column 2- Knave swords (reversed), 7 wands (upright), The World (upright)

Column 3- 8 cups (upright), The Tower (reversed), Queen wands (upright):

An interpretation: The first column, which represents the past, shows an abundance of hard work and opportunity in the Ace and the six, while the ten shows that there have been a lot of burdens that have been seen through to completion. In the center column, which represents the present, we see that there has been some hasty action, indicated by the reversed Knave, but also perseverance and completion. This contrast could be why the subject is feeling uneasy about making such a big transition. In the last column, which shows potential outcomes, the eight and the Tower show a lot of disappointment, stress, and upheaval, normal for a large transition such as a major move, but the upright Queen exudes confidence and determination. The subject may have a lot of apprehension about taking the new job and moving, but the cards indicate that despite the stress, hard work will lead to a positive outcome.

*The query: The subject is trying to determine the status of her love life. She loves her fiancé but isn't sure if she's ready for marriage.

Column 1- 5 wands (reversed), The Empress (upright), 2 swords (upright)

Column 2- 7 swords (upright), 3 wands (upright), The Devil (reversed)

Column 3- 2 pentacles (upright), 4 swords (reversed), Knight cups (upright):

An interpretation: This reading is related to a serious romantic commitment, and the first column shows that there have been a lot of conflicts and tough decisions made in the past, but that there has also been a lot of abundance and beauty to balance it out. In the center column, the cards show a bleak picture of the present, with betrayal and detachment featuring heavily, brightened only by the foresight depicted in the three of wands. The future column is not particularly cheery, either. It shows the split of priorities, as well as exhaustion and burn-out, which may occur if the subject goes ahead with planning her wedding with someone she's unsure about. The last card, the upright Knight, signifies opportunities and curiosity. This bride may want to take the cards' advice as suggesting she move on from her detached, draining relationship.

Celtic Cross

The Celtic Cross tarot layout is commonly used and can be one of the most effective if you use your intuition wisely. This layout is fairly simple to deal but takes a lot of practice to read effectively. We're putting it early in the chapter because we don't want you to be afraid of this layout, but want you to start using it because the more you use it, the more adept you will be. This is a great layout for those readings that are targeting a specific issue or question because it uses ten cards for a comprehensive view of what's going on with the subject of the reading. The cards can be read and explained individually, but the more practice you get, the more you will understand how the cards work together. When you become more intuitive, you'll be able to see the deal as the big picture.

You will shuffle and deal the ten cards in this order:

1- in the center of your reading space

2- laid diagonal across card #1

3- to the left of cards #1 and #2

4- to the right of cards #1 and #2

5- above cards #1 and #2

6- below cards #1 and #2

Thus, your cross is formed. To the right of the cross, you are going to deal cards #7-10 in a column, beginning at the bottom, so #7 is closest to you, finishing with # 10 on top of the column. The place where #8 and #9 meet should be online with the center of card #4. Each card is assigned an interpretive meaning:

1- the present

2- the challenge

These cards are connected because the challenge exists in the present part of the subject's life.

3- the past; it is to the left of #1 and #2 because it is behind the subject

4- the future; it is to the right of #1 and #2 because that is where the subject is looking

5- the above; this is what the subject aspires to

6- the below; this is what the subject's internal, subconscious feelings are

7- the advice; this card represents or suggests a potential solution

8- the external forces; this is the pressure the subject may feel from others

9- the hopes and fears; this is what is driving the subject or holding them back

10- the outcome; this card offers up the future based on the present course of action

Examples:

*The query: The subject is having trouble being an effective parent to her young children while dealing with upheaval at work. She wants to know if the two issues are related and how she can work to find a resolution.

1- Queen pentacles (upright)

2- 8 wands (upright)

3- 10 swords (reversed)

4- The Star (upright)

5- 8 pentacles (reversed)

6- Ace wands (reversed)

7- 9 cups (upright)

8- Temperance (upright)

9- King cups (reversed)

10- 4 pentacles (reversed)

An interpretation: The Queen and eight to open the deal represent the woman's talents and her issues with reconciling them to journey through motherhood and her career. The past and the future cards show that in the past, she had good health and optimism and that she can attain that again- meaning her present situation is difficult, but won't last forever. There is some negativity attached to her #5 and #6 cards, which show that outwardly and inwardly, there may be a desire to lose her ambition and determination. The upright nine in the advice position shows that the path to the future will need to include hope and an improvement in health, while Temperance and the reversed King show that the subject is being subjected to patience from the outside (definitely a good thing) but being held back by her internal demons. The reversed four in the outcome slot show that there will be obstacles unless something changes.

Although the subject asked about work/home balance, there is a heavy emphasis within these cards on physical and mental health. The subject should consider if there may be an underlying medical concern that may be driving her desire to fall back and step away from the chaos at home and work. A medical and mental health check-up might be in order to rule out anything that could be holding her back from finding balance and performing all her tasks satisfactorily.

*The query: The subject was recently widowed at a fairly young age. He is seeking guidance about handling grief and moving forward without his wife.

1- 5 pentacles (upright)

2- Knave cups (upright)

3- 9 wands (reversed)

4- Ace cups (upright)

5- 7 pentacles (reversed)

6- King wands (upright)

7- 6 swords (upright)

8- 2 wands (upright)

9- 5 cups (reversed)

10- Justice (upright)

An interpretation: This reading opens up appropriately enough with the five depicting despair and loneliness, and the concern card showing gentleness. This young widow is understandably sad, and his sensitive nature is making it difficult for him to make decisions moving forward. The past card shows illness, unsurprisingly, but the Ace in the future slot shows good health and joy. The aspirations and internal desires cards play out as impatience due to passion, which also falls in line with what we know about the subject. The advice card represents both sorrow and a journey, which seems to be pointing to the journey of grief, with the pressure card and the hopes and fears card indicating patience, courage, and hope. The outcome card indicates harmony and balance to be found honorably.

This reading is overwhelmingly positive regarding this young widower's concerns. Although he may be suffering grief at his loss, the cards have shown him that there will be light and joy on the far side of his journey and that he just needs to accept the hope and patience of others around him and he will be okay. He has permission to grieve and then move on with his life.

Horseshoe (7)

The 7-card horseshoe is a simple layout that can help with decision-making. After shuffling, you'll deal out the first card closest to you at the left and then deal in an arc, creating a horseshoe, with the #4 card at the top, and the #7 card closest to you on the right. Like the Celtic Cross, each card in the horseshoe deal is assigned a meaning. The cards should be read in their dealt order to create a comprehensive picture of the subject's query.

1- the past

2- the present

3- the future

4- the attitude toward the question/decision

5- the other/outside influences

6- the obstacles

7- the outcome

Examples:

*The query: The subject wants to understand her career path and if she's made the best choices to achieve her goals.

1- 4 cups (upright)

2- The Hermit (upright)

3- Queen wands (reversed)

4- 6 pentacles (upright)

5- 9 swords (upright)

6- 6 wands (reversed)

7- Knight pentacles (reversed)

An interpretation: The cards show that the subject dealt with being unsatisfied in the past, causing a reevaluation that led to caution moving forward into the present. However, the reversed Queen in the future slot shows that there is the potential for jealousy and vengefulness on the horizon. Since the subject is concerned about her career path, this may give her pause about the decisions she is contemplating, but the upright six in the attitude slot shows that the subject is giving of her talents, despite a suspicion of her motives coming from the outside. The obstacles and outcome slots indicate that there may be a slowdown or postponement in the advancement of riches.

Given the negative connotation of the latter cards, the subject may want to rethink the decisions she is making surrounding her career advancement. It's possible that her giving nature may be seen as a ruse and that she would be subjected to bias, career slowdowns, or loss of opportunity based on the suspicions and jealousy of others.

*The query: The subject is contemplating making a major purchase and needs guidance on decision-making.

1- 5 swords (reversed)

2- 10 pentacles (upright)

3- Queen swords (upright)

4- 3 cups (upright)

5- The Chariot (reversed)

6- 8 swords (reversed)

7- 4 pentacles (upright)

An interpretation: This reading is interesting because it revolves around the best use of wealth. The past and present cards indicate that the subject had suffered loss and disappointment in the past, but is currently enjoying wealth and prosperity. The upright Queen in the future shows that the subject will be seen as skillful and clever, signifying that it may be a good time to make a major investment. The middle cards show that even though the subject has a good attitude about his fortune, those looking in may still see him as unsuccessful. The obstacles and outcome cards indicate that there may be accusations of greed despite the freedom that wealth brings to the subject.

The cards here lean towards telling the subject that it's okay to make his large purchase and enjoy his wealth, but that there may be detractors. It's up to the subject to determine whether or not he cares about the opinions of others and if he feels the need to justify how he spends his hard-earned money.

Horseshoe (5)

The five-card horseshoe is used for more generalized readings, ones that can help your subject understand more about themselves and their relationship with the greater world. As with the 7-card horseshoe, you will deal the cards in an arc from left to right. The meanings assigned to these cards is as follows:

1- the current situation

2- the path ahead

3- the heart

4- the near future

5- the far future

Examples:

*The query: An older subject has been in conflict with her son about his plans after college, and wants to know if and how they will be able to find family harmony again.

1- 3 swords (upright)

2- 9 pentacles (upright)

3- Knight wands (reversed)

4- Two cups (upright)

5- The Hanged Man (reversed)

An interpretation: This reading starts appropriately enough with the upright three signifying a broken relationship or inner conflict, but the path card shows well-being ahead. The Knight indicates that there is closed-mindedness at play and that the near future and far future are at odds between fruitless sacrifice and familial cooperation.

These cards indicate a deep-seated issue that may not be easily resolved. It would appear that those involved are determined that their way is the 'right' way, and until communications and minds can become more open, the conflict will continue.

*The query: A young man needs guidance on choosing between taking a job near home or accepting one in another country.

1- Queen cups (reversed)

2- The Moon (reversed)

3- 3 pentacles (upright)

4- 10 cups (upright)

5- Ace wands (upright)

An interpretation: The current situation shown by these cards isn't a happy one- it indicates that there is a gloom hanging over the subject. The reversed Moon isn't much happier, showing that there may be deception and mistakes ahead. The heart card gets to the meat of the issue; it depicts that the subject may be having a hard time with his decision because he is seeking approval and wants to display his true abilities. There is some light for this subject, though, as both the near and far future slots show that there is happiness, love, and a profitable new beginning ahead.

This reading indicates that the subject needs to think about why he is seeking approval and from whom he is seeking it. If the job in the new country is something that will get him away from an atmosphere where he is stuck in a cycle of seeking approval that never comes, these cards seem to be pointing to that path- the one that will lead him to a happier, freer existence.

Five-Card Spread

The five-card layout is a left to right straight-line deal that helps your subject examine their past and decide a path for the future. It's as simple as it sounds; just shuffle and deal five cards left to right. Each card is read individually and then put together into an intuitive story. The meanings are as follows:

1- the far past

2- the near past

3- the present

4- the near future

5- the far future

Examples:

*The query: A married couple is seeking guidance on how to approach their retirement years.

1- Ace swords (upright)

2- King pentacles (reversed)

3- 4 wands (reversed)

4- Strength (upright)

5- 7 cups (upright)

An interpretation: A look at the cards signifying this couple's past shows that they are in a loving relationship, but have more recently fallen prey to materialism. This may be at the root of their difficulty in deciding the future of their retirement. Their present card does show that they are game for new adventures, which bodes well for them to come together on a set plan. Their near and far future cards are a bit of a mixed bag, however, showing that there is courage and conviction up ahead, but also the chance of losing direction.

If these subjects are to be able to choose their retirement path, they are going to have to get their ambitions on the same page to avoid one or the other being unhappy with the results. They need to weigh their options and make sure they agree, or they will end up drifting closer to retirement without a set plan.

*The query: A young man is trying to choose what college to attend.

1- Knave swords (upright)

2- Death (upright)

3- 4 pentacles (upright)

4- 10 swords (reversed)

5- 8 wands (reversed)

An interpretation: This subject might be alarmed at seeing the Death card in his deal, but in this case, it represents a transformation. Along with the Knave, signifying grace and diplomacy, this seems to indicate that the subject is well-heeled as he transitions into the next stage of his life. The four in the present slot is disconcerting, as this card usually depicts greed and lack of generosity, but in the case of this reading, it may directly relate to the inability to get funding from one of his college choices. The good news is that the near and far future cards show both indicate courage, with the ten signifying positive energy.

This reading seems to be telling the subject that he needs to think about which option will be the best for him in terms of health and happiness and not in terms of money. The positivity shown by the future cards indicates that he will succeed if he makes the choice that is best for his long-term well-being.

Five-by-Two Spread

This spread builds upon the last single-row deal. Instead of using one line of five cards, you'll expand to two rows. This layout is generally used to help a subject determine the path of their life over the course of the following year. You'll deal this layout in columns of two, so #1, #3, #5, #7, and #9 will be the top row, and #2, #4, #6, #8, and #10 will be the bottom row. Deal the cards in order, top to bottom first, then left to right. The meanings for each column should be interpreted as:

1,2- the present condition and circumstances

3,4- the hopes, wishes, and fears of the subject

5,6- unexpected circumstances that may occur during the year

7,8- potential short-term outcomes

9,10- potential long-term outcomes

Examples:

*The query: A young couple is looking for advice about whether or not to try to start a family this year.

<u>1- 7 wands (upright)</u>

2- The Emperor (upright)

3- 6 cups (reversed)

4- Knight pentacles (upright)

5- 4 wands (upright)

6- 8 cups (upright)

7- 10 wands (reversed)

8- 2 swords (reversed)

9- 9 pentacles (upright)

10- Wheel of Fortune (upright)

An interpretation: This reading starts appropriately enough with a seven signifying courage and energy, and the Emperor depicting the establishment of patriarchy, giving an accurate picture of the subjects' circumstances. The hopes and fears column displays a mix of apprehension regarding potential disappointments and the positivity of the trust between the couple. The center column shows that the fear of disappointment may be real and that there may be a need for reevaluation as the year progresses. The near future cards indicate that there will be a renewed sense of energy and release, while the long-term future cards show that there will be progress, unexpected events, and eventual well-being.

The cards seem to be telling the subjects that no matter how much they love each other, this year might not be the best to start a family. If there is going to be pain and disappointment mid-year, but well-being at the end of the year, they may want to wait until then to begin trying for a pregnancy. This reading could also indicate that trying for pregnancy early in the year could end in disappointment or sorrow (perhaps a miscarriage?), and that may give them the impetus to wait a while until the timing seems better.

*The query: An older businessman is seeking guidance on taking his retirement, selling his company, or continuing to work.

1- 4 swords (reversed)

2- Knight swords (reversed)

3- 6 wands (upright)

4- 10 pentacles (upright)

5- The Magician (upright)

6- Ace wands (reversed)

7- 5 pentacles (upright)

8- 7 cups (upright)

9- 8 wands (reversed)

10- King swords (reversed)

An interpretation: The present circumstances represented in this deal seem to show a certain amount of unrest and oppression, but the hopes and fears column is more positive, indicating that the subject has faith in his past successes and the stability of his wealth. The obstacles column depicts that there may be deceit and a lack of direction, which means that the subject might be taken for a victim within his own organization. The short-term future cards aren't much more positive, indicating a lack of direction and loneliness. The far future column shows violence and bad intentions.

Given the negativity of the cards, the deal seems to signify that the subject should consider staying in his business and cleaning up the potential messes before he considers selling or retiring. It would seem that bad actors are hiding within the business or his business network waiting to pounce and destroy what he's built, and it's in his best interest to consider staying, for now, to root out the negative parties and protect his livelihood and legacy.

Twelve-Card General Spread

The last layout we'll talk about is a spread that can be used to help a subject get a good handle on what the tarot has to say about their personality and decision-making skills. This is, like the Celtic Cross, a very intuitive layout. The more you practice this layout, the better you will become at interpreting it. Each card has a specific spot in the deal, and it's easier to show you than to list the positions:

1   2   3   6   7   4   5   8   9

10   11   12

You will shuffle and deal the cards in the order shown above. Each card has as assigned interpretation, as follows:

1- a signifier card, showing the core of the subject's personality

2- the mind

3- the body

4- the spirit

5- family and friends

6- romance

7- hobbies

8- careers

9- finances

10- blessings

11- challenges

12- advice

Examples:

*The query: A man who has been unlucky in personal relationships wants to discover more about himself, so he can determine why he is unsuccessful in matters of love.

1- 2 wands (upright)

2- 8 swords (upright)

3- King pentacles (upright)

4-10 cups (reversed)

5- The Fool (reversed)

6- 5 wands (upright)

7- Knight cups (upright)

8- 3 cups (reversed)

9- The Lovers (upright)

10- 6 swords (reversed)

11- 8 pentacles (upright)

12-Queen wands (upright)

An interpretation: The signifier card here shows that the subject is a person with a generous heart and spirit. This will play heavily into the rest of the reading, as the subject has specifically focused on his romantic prospects. The mind card indicates indecision and weakness, so it's possible the subject may come across as wishy-washy to potential partners. The King in the body slot shows that the subject is perceived as steady and reliable. The spirit card indicates broken relationships and quarrels, perhaps a remnant in the reading of the subject's previous experiences.

Moving into the next third of the deal, the family and friends card shows the reversed Fool, signifying hesitation, apathy, and injustice. It's feasible that the subject doesn't have a functional family life, which could be why he's unsure of how to pursue healthy romantic relationships. The romance card, which is the focal point of this reading, shows a propensity for quarreling- again, an indicator that the subject may be unsure of how to act in a relationship or what a healthy relationship is supposed to look like.

As far as hobbies and careers are concerned, these cards are a bit on the negative side. They indicate shyness and lack of communication, which might depict difficulties relating to others in social settings and at work, but there is a note of hope in the Knight, which represents emotional intelligence. The presence of the Lovers in the finances slot bodes well for the subject, as it appears he is doing well monetarily, although the reversed six in the blessings slot does show that there are obstacles and defeat on the way to happiness.

The reading does end on a high note as the challenges card seems to denote that the obstacles shown by the previous card can be overcome with hard work. The last card, the upright Queen, shows command and affection. This indicates that the subject will have to conquer his communication issues, but once he does, he will be able to learn what a healthy relationship looks like and be able to find fulfilling romance in the future. The subject should focus on improving his outlook on himself, grow his confidence in his communications, and then look for love. Until he does so, he'll continue to be stuck in the same pattern of failed romances.

*The query: A pair of sisters have historically been close, but find themselves in conflict and growing apart recently. They are seeking advice about repairing their relationship and want to know what they should be working on.

1- 10 swords (upright)

2- King wands (upright)

3- 3 swords (reversed)

4- 7 pentacles (upright)

5- 5 cups (upright)

6- The Sun (upright)

7- 3 wands (reversed)

8- Queen cups (reversed)

9- 6 pentacles (upright)

10- 2 cups (upright)

11- The High Priestess (reversed)

12- 9 swords (reversed)

An interpretation: This is an interesting reading because it's two subjects asking about their relationship, not just a single subject looking for advice. To handle this reading, the signifier card will apply to the nature of the relationship, not one individual. To that end, the signifier here shows that these sisters are currently in a state of pain and distrust. The upright King in their mind slot does indicate that they have passionate and noble ideals, while the body card shows that the relationship is marred by sorrow and confusion. There's good news in the spirit card though; it indicates that the relationship is built on hard work and can be re-evaluated.

In the next section of the deal, the family card becomes the focal point of the reading, as it indicates a broken marriage, mistrust, and sorrow. Maybe the subjects' relationship has been negatively affected by the collapse of family relationships around them. The Sun in the romance slot gives hope that the sisters can find happiness in love again, either with partners or with each other, as the romance card can deal with all matters of love, not just romantic love. The reversed cards in the hobbies and careers slots seem to indicate that the subjects are no longer enjoying activities that they used to enjoy together due to mistrust, perceived slights, and arrogance. It would seem the sisters have fallen out of favor with each other but aren't talking about why, instead choosing to let their hurt feelings drive them farther apart.

The last section of the reading bodes well for the subjects, at least in the department of finances and blessings, which indicate charity, prosperity, and cooperation. Apropos of the circumstance, the reversed High Priestess shows that the subjects will face the challenges of misunderstanding and selfishness, but the reversed nine shows then the path to healing through being unselfish and sharing encouraging news. Overall, this reading indicates that the subjects are letting misunderstanding, miscommunication, and a heavy focus on their own feelings over the other's stand in the way of what was once a close relationship. These sisters need to begin listening to and taking care of each other again, and their relationship will heal and be renewed.

##

As you can see from all these sample deals and interpretations, the cards all work together to tell a story for the subject. The more you deal, read, and practice, the more adept you will become at being an intuitive storyteller. As we go through the rest of this section, we'll talk about intuition, reading the cards and the subjects, protecting yourself from emotional projection, and developing your personal style with the cards.

Additional Notes About Methods for Dealing

When you are dealing your cards, you may choose to lay them out all at once so that each card is face-up on the table when you begin your reading. This is a good way to deal a set of cards that you are going to be reading and interpreting as a whole. If you are going to be reading each card individually, you may choose to deal and interpret them on at a time so that you aren't influenced by the sight of the other card and can focus on each card's meanings. You can then put the meanings together at the end to complete your reading.

You should shuffle the cards and cut or ask the subject to cut them before dealing, and you should always pause to reflect on the intention of the reading, or the question being asked of the cards before you deal. This will direct your mental and emotional energy into your deck and clear your mind of all other distractions. Focus and intention are crucial to accurate readings. You want to communicate to your subject that you are fully present in the task and are giving them your best efforts. Your subject should always feel that you are invested in helping them work through their questions and concerns.

As you progress in your dealing and reading skills, you might find that you want to keep the Major Arcana out of the deck before you shuffle and deal. You can draw a Major Arcana card to be a signifier card to determine the role or mindset of the subject. Set it aside, face down, and then shuffle the rest of the Major Arcana back into the deck and proceed with the rest of the layout process. When you are done, you can flip and interpret the signifier card and use that as a basis for the rest of the reading. The more you practice, the more you will develop your own sense of style when it comes to dealing and laying out the cards. You'll come to find that you've got favorite and less-favored layouts, and you may even create adaptations of some existing layouts to find ones that work best for you and your skills.

If you're a visual learner, you may want to search online for videos of tarot layouts. You can watch different styles of shuffling, cutting, and dealing to see what appeals to you. You might see someone deal in a style you admire and want to emulate. You may find some new layouts to try. What you will definitely see is people bucking against the stereotype of who reads tarot. We're going to spend a lot of time talking about that when we get to Part IV of this book. The important point here is that with time and practice, you will develop a style that works for you and is all your own.

Reading People When Reading the Cards

One of the most important elements of being a capable and intuitive tarot reader is being able to also read your subjects. You must use your emotional intelligence, empathy, and social awareness to excel at reading tarot. Many tarot readers are, by nature, empaths. Empaths are in tune with the feelings of those around them, often to their own detriment because they can get overwhelmed with emotional energy if they don't know how to protect themselves. If you believe that you may be an empath, you may want to look into empath training, so that you can study important techniques for guarding yourself against being overcome with the emotional energy of others. We'll go over a couple of simple methods a little later in this segment so you can learn the basics.

Whether you're an empath or just highly intuitive, you need to apply those skills to your tarot reading. You will encounter three main types of reading subjects. Some people are vested in the cards and will take your interpretation as gospel. Others will take a more practical approach, and see the cards for what they are- a guide and tool for decision-making and contemplation. The last group will be skeptics. They want to see what you can do before they believe. You should be able to tell which of the three types you are dealing with before you begin.

When you are talking with your subject about their question or appeal, listen carefully to what they are saying and watch them carefully for what they are not saying. Being able to read body language is important. Once they've laid out their appeal to you, ask thoughtful questions, based on what they've said and how they've acted. People who are looking for guidance may be stressed out, which can present as tense shoulders, hand-wringing, leg-bouncing, and/or the use of verbal crutches when they are trying to express their concerns to you. Pay close attention to these behaviors. They can tell you a lot about the mindset of your subject before you've even dealt a single card.

Asking your subject questions helps you determine helpful information that will aid you in creating an accurate picture for them once you've dealt the cards. If you are reading the cards with someone who is skeptical ("Aren't the cards supposed to tell you everything?"), you can explain that the more details you have, the more detailed your reading will be. Asking questions also shows your subject that you are listening, that you care, and that you are taking on their concern as your own. Talk to your subject between cards and take into account what they are saying and how their demeanor changes as you explain the cards. You need to learn to read their emotions in real-time as you read the deck.

If it's someone's first reading, you want to assure them that the cards are a tool and not some sort of omniscient being. It's important that people know that a reading is to be used as a guide and does not represent an immovable outcome. The subject has free will to use the reading for their benefit, and that its purpose is to lend a depth of insight to the past and present, and to reveal what the potential is for the future. Once the reading is done, the subject is free to use the information given to them in any way that they see fit. Your subjects should know this before you begin. They should also be asked to keep their minds focused on the intent of their query or appeal during the reading. The more energy concentrated on the cards, the more accurate the reading will be.

No matter what mood your reading begins and ends with, you should always keep a calm, sympathetic demeanor. Sometimes people get excited or upset over the cards laid before them. If you maintain an even tone of voice, offer encouragement, and don't hesitate as you interpret, you will convey to your subject that the cards are not good or bad, they just are. It's okay to be thoughtful about your interpretations and offer the different meanings of the cards, but you shouldn't pause indecisively or use verbal crutches. You want to express your confidence in the cards and your interpretation skills to the subject of your reading. If you hold to a calm, kind, firm tone, you will set the mood for you, the subject, and the interpretation.

After a while, you'll become adept at recognizing who is going to live and die by the cards, and you can try to mitigate your readings with calm language to assuage any unnecessary dramatics. You will have subjects who will take everything the cards say at face value and, for lack of a better term, freak out. Stay calm- it is against your principles, or shall we say, tarot ethics for what it's worth- to let someone become overcome with hysteria over the cards. Keep your tone even and firm, and let your subject know they should be quietly focusing their energy on the query. Reassure them that you are interpreting the cards as accurately as you can, and even if a negative card comes up, it's all a part of the big picture.

Practice will never make 'perfect' when it comes to reading tarot and reading people, but the more you practice, the more intuitive you will become. You will become more comfortable with the cards, and studying the meanings will help you smooth out your readings. When you don't need to constantly pause to think about the meanings of the individual cards, you will be able to create larger, more accurate interpretations for your subjects. Read up and quiz yourself on card meanings. Practice shuffling and dealing smoothly. Have a few close friends or family members that will let you read for them regularly, whether they believe in the cards or not. Just being able to practice your deals and your demeanor will be tremendously beneficial. You may even win over their skepticism in the meantime.

If you *are* empathic and find yourself being overcome with the emotional energy of others, then you need to learn a couple of basic techniques to avoid being drained. Whitelighting is a common method used by empaths to protect themselves from being overwhelmed in what may be an overly emotional situation. It's a handy technique for events like weddings and funerals and can protect against an onslaught of emotion in any everyday setting. It's especially useful for guarding yourself while giving tarot readings.

White lighting is simple and only requires a few minutes and your powers of concentration. Sitting or standing with your spine straight, as if you were being suspended by a string at the crown of your head, imagine a ball of light hovering over you. Now, visualize that light coming down over your head and slowly moving over you all the way down to your toes. This light is your protection. It will keep a shield around you while you go about your business. You want to imagine its warmth like a secure hug keeping the world at bay.

When you feel an overwhelming emotion creeping in, close your eyes for a moment, and picture the light. When you've finished needing your white light, concentrate again and let it recede from your feet back up over your body and out the top of your head. Some people like to white light in the opposite direction, with the light originating from the ground to cover them from toe to head. Whichever direction you are more comfortable with is fine.

Another way to guard against unwanted, overwhelming emotions is to ground yourself before beginning a reading. Make sure you have your feet planted firmly on the floor, and closing your eyes, take a few deep breaths. Concentrate on the connection between your body and the ground. Meditate on your intention to stay focused on that connection. When you are done and you begin the tarot reading, keep your feet touching the floor at all times, so you do not break the connection. After the reading is done and you no longer need the grounding, you can break the link, but be sure to do so with purpose. Empaths have a unique bond with the earth's electromagnetic energy. Grounding taps into that energy for strength.

One other thing that works well for empaths and non-sensitive people alike is the use of crystals. These rocks and gems all have obligate powers and by keeping the right ones near you or on your person during a tarot reading, you can tap into their strengths to guide you and protect yourself from overwhelming emotions. Some popular crystals are black tourmaline, which protects from being overcome with negativity, amethyst to rid your space of bad energy, green calcite, which provides and promotes calm, and agate, which reinforces the energy flow between people and the earth. The use of crystals is a science of itself, and there are many guides and videos available to help you decide what's best for you.

Go with Your Gut

We've talked a lot about intuition. It is a crucial part of taking your tarot readings from dry interpretation to rich, story-telling divinations. Chances are good that if you're taking up reading tarot, you're either an empath (as mentioned in the last segment), or you have a good 'gut.' We hear the phrase "what does your gut tell you?" pretty frequently when it comes to making important decisions or analyzing first impressions. A gut feeling is an unshakable sense that comes from your core. You might not be able to explain exactly what it is, but you just *know* the right answer.

For a lot of people who have recently discovered that they are sensitive or empathic, the tarot deck provides the perfect outlet for them to use their gifts. The intuitive nature of empaths and sensitives is perfectly designed for the art of tarot. If you aren't in one of these categories, you might have to work a little harder at developing intuition, but it's not impossible. Just as we learned to read people in the last segment, you can learn to read yourself, too, and that's what intuition really is. It's the ability to take in everything going on around you and within you, and trusting yourself to make the right decision or judgment call based on your observations.

When you're reading the tarot cards, you have to trust your gut. This means in regard to the cards and the subject of the reading. You are obligated to be truthful to the subject and read the cards accurately and to the best of your ability. However, you are also obligated to be kind. This means that you should in no way lie, or lie by omission, about the cards to spare someone's feelings, but find a way to deliver your interpretation gently. If the cards are portraying something negative, you need to share that interpretation, but do it kindly and firmly, especially if it seems like your subject is going to be upset by the reading. By trusting your eyes, your emotional intelligence, and your gut, you will soon find the best way to impart the information from the cards to your subject.

If you *are* empathic, you're going to get hit with a whammy of emotions if the reading skews towards either end of the scale. If someone is upset over a reading with a lot of negative implications, steel yourself for that onslaught of negative energy. If someone ends up with a particularly positive reading, you will also feel a rush of joy. Don't let these external emotions cloud your judgment as you finish the reading. Let your gut take the lead and leave your heart out of it. The cards themselves are not inherently good or bad- it's the energy that is put into and taken from them that dictates what the mood will be before, during, and after a reading. Use your protection techniques to avoid too many emotional highs and lows. Too much energy from other people's emotions can be draining and detrimental to your well-being.

Even if you're not an empath, it can be hard not to get caught up in the emotion of the subject as you are performing your reading. You don't want to seem unfeeling, but you can't let someone else's emotions dictate or sway how you read the cards. It can be tough, especially if the reading isn't showing particularly good news. It can be tempting to try to bring the interpretation back around to the positive, but you are in a position where you must be accurate and truthful, or you will lose credibility as a tarot reader. Many of your subjects will be in the first two categories that we talked about earlier- the hardcore believers and the pragmatists. They will know if you are fudging their reading to skew towards the positive. Don't give in to that temptation.

When you're performing a tarot reading, the assumption from the subject, whether an aficionado or a first-time skeptic, is that you know what you are talking about. And you should. Studying the cards and their meanings is a lot of hard work, but it will pay off in the end. Once you've committed the meanings to memory, you will be able to go with your gut feeling as you interpret the cards with ease and fluidity. It's all about proficiency, intuition, and storytelling ability. You will improve in all these areas with time and practice.

Developing Your Signature Style

As you progress in your tarot reading skills, you are also going to be developing your style. The tarot should be as personal to you as it is to the subjects who wish to have their cards read. You will find a ton of ways to make your style your own, from choosing decks that appeal to you aesthetically to finding your unique reading voice and flair. If you want to make a business out of tarot, which we will delve into in Part IV, you may want to go for a certain style of dress or choose a signature color to wear for your readings. This can make you stand out and give you a bit of a brand, one which you might want to parlay into a tarot business later on.

We talked a little earlier about watching videos of other tarot readers to get an idea of what appeals to you and what doesn't. You can also take the time to have your own cards read by established tarot readers and pay attention not only to how they deal and interpret the cards but also how they speak and act. You will have a front-row seat to see how others handle their cards and their layouts, including whether or not they lay all the cards face up, or flip them one at a time for dramatic effect or to keep their judgment unclouded as they interpret each card. As you've probably figured out by now, there is no exact right or wrong way to handle your tarot cards, as long as you stay true to the meanings and interpretations.

Preparing and Cleansing Your Cards

One important thing to remember is that the cards, which are inanimate objects, are affected by the energy of the people around them. Much like an empath needs to shield themselves from overwhelming emotion, so too do the cards need to be protected. When you get a new deck of cards, you need to make them your own. Carry them around close to your body. Meditate on your good intentions for your new cards. Shuffle and handle them to put your energy into the cards. When it's time to perform a reading, concentrate on your intentions for that session, and give your energy to the deck.

When you are done with a reading, you can care for your cards by cleansing them of the previous energy. There are a few different methods you can use for cleansing your deck:

1) Sort your deck back into an upright position, and put the cards in order- Major Arcana, Wands, Cups, Swords, Pentacles. Once this is done (and you know all your cards are there!), shuffle them vigorously seven times. Think positive thoughts and put good energy back into the cards before storing them.

2) Sort your cards and light a smudge stick or sage incense. Hold your deck together and pass it lightly through the smoke from the smudge or the incense. Take care not to singe your cards- don't hold them too close to the hot end of the smudge or the incense.

3) Sort your deck and pack your cards in salt. Place the cards in a tightly sealed bag and place them in a large airtight container of salt, completely buried. The salt will draw bad energy out of the deck and form a protective shield for your next reading. For maximum effect, leave the cards buried for at least three or four days and up to a week.

4) Use a full moon bath. When the moon is full, place your cards in a window or safely outdoors where they can bathe in the moon's beams. This cleans away any negative energy and leaves your cards at neutral. You can also give your cards a sunbath to imbue them with warmth and positivity.

Some tarot readers like to sort and shuffle for cleansing in between every reading, especially if the subject chose to cut the cards and imbued their energy into your deck. You can choose to do this frequent cleansing, or you may want to do a more thorough cleanse after a particularly emotional or negative reading. It's up to you- only you can feel the energy of your cards. You will know when your deck's energy is out of line, and only you can decide how best to restore its balance.

Phew- we hope you've stuck with us through all this information! It's been a lot of fun to go through the card meanings and sample readings and talk about layouts and learning to use your intuition. You can come back to this part of the book to study and refresh yourself whenever you need a boost. In the last part, we'll be talking about modern applications of tarot, tarot as it's portrayed in popular culture, how to handle skeptics and stereotypes to be a tarot reader in the 21st-century, and how to preserve and promote the art of tarot for generations to come.

PART IV
Tarot In The Modern World

Tarot, which has come a long way from its roots as a card game, is still very much in use and evolving. There are digital platforms and a global communication network that allow the reading of tarot to be available to anyone seeking instruction or guidance. So, that begs the question that we'll address in our first section here- who is using tarot in the 21st century?

Who Still Uses Tarot?

Tarot has been in continual usage for the last few centuries, and it shows no signs of going away. The internet plays a huge role in the art of tarot these days, with readers and subjects being able to connect online for virtual readings and lessons on interpretation. It's easier than ever to order and receive decks through online shopping and mail-order- a vast evolution from the days of hand-made, hand-cut cards, or even the need to find an occult shop, which today are, sadly, few and far between.

You might be surprised at who uses tarot, and we'll talk about stereotypes shortly, but the truth is that tarot readers and subjects come from every demographic. Many people, tired of the everyday grind, seek comfort in the cards as they look for guidance on making difficult decisions. For others, reading tarot is a family tradition, passed down from generations as both an amusing diversion and a divination tool. Others still use tarot as a business or side business, using their skills for profit. Tarot has also become a popular addition for people who practice regular meditation, using one or two cards every day as the subject of their reflections.

The use of tarot is a personal decision, and your reason for practicing the art may be wildly different from each and every other tarot reader you meet. There is one common thread between each reader and every person who seeks to have their cards read, and that is the desire to connect with something beyond the mundane- the very definition of the occult.

Some Notes on Self-Reading

It's a popular activity among tarot readers to read their own cards both for practice and for guidance. Reading your own cards strengthens your bond to your deck and reinforces your interpretation skills. You can draw a card each morning to be your intention for the day, which is also a terrific way to familiarize yourself with the deck. You can also give yourself a full reading one or two times a week to study and learn as well as give yourself guidance. Try keeping a tarot journal to determine patterns in your self-readings- this will give you additional insight into what's going on with your own life. There's no use being a tarot reader if you can't use your craft on yourself, right?

The one thing about self-reading, though, is that it can become boring. You know who you are and what your hopes and aspirations are. You know what's going on in your own life, and the cards are either going to reinforce things you already know, or you may find yourself in the unhealthy habit of skewing the cards to say what you want them to say. Try and guard against self-bias. If you have a close friend or family member who also reads tarot, you should read each other's cards when you can to avoid putting too much of your own energy into the readings.

While it can be useful to read your own cards when the occasion calls for it, it's much better to practice reading the cards of other people if you want to become adept at being a smooth, intuitive storyteller. Remember that you're not only learning to read the cards, but also the people whose cards you are reading. The subject, their query, and their emotions are just as important as the cards themselves.

Can Belief Become Too Strong?

The cards, as we've previously discussed, are a tool. They are, in the end, pieces of brightly colored cardboard and do not have any power on their own. The cards are imbued with the energy of their owner- you, the reader- and the subject and the intent of their query. But can that link become too strong? Can people become too reliant on the cards to 'tell them' what to do?

In a way, the answer is yes. Tarot can become addictive, and we use that word in the most scientific sense. An addiction occurs when the brain's neural pathways are changed based on a chemical response in the synapses. When the reward center of the brain is activated regularly, the cells themselves come to expect and thrive upon the thing that activated them. This is how drug and alcohol dependencies develop, as well as dependencies on activities like playing video games or watching TV. It's not always a negative addiction- it can be things like the phenomenon of the runner's high. It all boils down to the way the human brain responds to stimulation of its rewards center.

As a tarot reader, it is up to you to explain the purpose of the cards to those who want their cards read. It's also up to you to know whether you should ethically read someone's cards on a more-than-frequent basis. You may be dealing with a subject who believes that the cards are a definitive predictor of the future and that there can be no deviation from the shown outcome. It's possible that the subject is trying to handle personal issues so big that they are grasping for anything that might offer hope. You should use your judgment on a case-by-case basis and once again, go with your gut.

It's okay to say, "You know, Mrs. Smith, we just read your cards yesterday. We should take some time between readings to see how things play out." Coming from you, the trusted tarot reader, Mrs. Smith might be convinced to wait for a few days between queries. If you think that Mrs. Smith may need assistance in other areas, and you know her well enough, you might ask if there's a different query you can help her with. Knowing when to help, when to back off, and when to humor your regulars is something that will develop along with your intuition about the cards.

If you've ever worked as a bartender or restaurant server, you've likely had to use your intuition about people who've been consuming alcohol. How did you figure out what the best course of action was when someone had been drinking a little too much? You would cut them off if they'd had too, too much, of course. If they were a little intoxicated but not to the point of being harmed or being harmful, you'd check and make sure they weren't driving anywhere or finding them a cab. If they seemed okay, you'd just go about your business. You knew who the 'problem' drinkers were and weren't. It's the same when you are a tarot reader. You need to give people what's in their best interests while performing your duties and keeping your integrity. So while yes, people can become "addicted" to having their cards read, remember that you, as the reader, have control over how much you are comfortable with letting them consume.

Handling Skepticism

As a proud tarot reader, you are going to run across your fair share of skepticism. People will scoff that they're just cards. That's true. The cards are an inanimate object. The power and energy come from you. When you run across a skeptic, there are a couple of things you can do, and you should always do them with kindness and respect. Take the high road at all times, because you don't want to do anything to prove your skeptic right about his misconceptions of tarot readers.

Show, Don't Tell

When you're dealing with a skeptic, the first thing you can do is offer a reading. Instead of telling someone about the power and art of tarot, you can show them. Of course, you should never force someone into a reading (that's just asking for a ton of bad energy!), but often skeptics on any topic or belief will enter into the activity they are arguing against just to prove the other person wrong. In this case, the skeptic may say, "Sure- read my cards, they're going to be a bunch of nonsense!"

That's great, isn't it? Time to do your thing. Ask them if there is something specific that they'd like to know about. Go through a basic reading with them, concentrating on their energy and on the cards. Don't rush or allow yourself to be unnerved by their disbelief. You will strike a chord during the reading, guaranteed. That's the beautiful thing about the tarot cards. When used with purpose and imbued with good intent, there is something for everyone to be found within the deck. Don't expect an epiphany right before your eyes, although if your skeptic has a light bulb moment, it's worth celebrating. It's more likely that they will leave the reading without a visible change in attitude.

Why? Because when you don't believe in something and then you are proven to be mistaken, it can take a little while for the realization to sink in. Your skeptic might go about their business, still scoffing, until they start to think. It could be while taking a drive, washing up in the shower, or sitting at the bar talking to a friend, but eventually, they'll say, "Huh. That's what the tarot reader was talking about!"

Your words and your interpretation will affect the skeptic; it's just a matter of when. You may never see that person again to know that you've helped change their mind, or they may begin coming to you regularly for readings. There's no guarantee either way. But by showing rather than telling, you've given the skeptic food for thought and proven yourself as a skilled, passionate reader.

Be Open-Minded

Some people are so set against anything occult that they will rail vehemently against the thought of a reading. If they're against having their cards read, but not against having a conversation, ask them what you can do to help them understand. Be calm and be the voice for your art. Explain that the cards are just an object, but it's the reader that makes them work. You can talk about your spiritual path to becoming a tarot reader and why you choose to practice the cards.

Ask the skeptic about their hobbies and why they choose to pursue them. Exchange ideas and find common ground. The more you talk to a skeptic, the more commonalities you may find. If they have a crafty hobby, you can show them the similarities between putting your energy into a piece of art and putting your energies into telling a story with the cards. You can talk about your 'origin stories' to see if their art and your art both came from similar beginnings, such as a family tradition or something you took up after a traumatic event. Even if you cannot convince a hardcore skeptic that the cards are a valid, practicable art form, you should be able to find a peaceable agreement that to each, their own.

Tarot On TV- Handling Stereotypes and Pop Culture Misconceptions

Let's be frank; pop culture is often unkind to tarot readers. If you're easily offended, you might want to skip over this segment because we're going to be raw and honest about some terms that some people may not want to hear. This is solely for the purpose of historical context, and we promise this in no way reflects our personal values. We believe that tarot stereotypes are made to be broken, and that tarot should be accessible to all who wish to practice and participate in readings.

One of the tropes that comes to mind is that of the 'gypsy' fortune teller, sitting in a darkened wagon, tapestries hung all about, seated on a small velvet table, beckoning you to see what your future holds. We've seen this scenario in countless old movies and TV programs. To start debunking this stereotype, the first thing to point out is that the Romany people take high offense to the 'g' word, and if you are confronted with it by a skeptic or naysayer, you should call them out right away and politely but firmly ask that they do NOT use that word again.

Once that's out of the way, you should point out that the tarot cards don't tell the future; they tell what could *potentially* happen in the future. Explain that people who have their cards read need to take the reading as advice or guidance, not as a fixed outcome that isn't affected by free will. Third, while the Romany people did and continue to use the tarot for divination, this is more an expression and extension of their spirituality. It's long been believed by many that the Romany have a deep connection with the esoteric and the earth, and indeed, a large number among their population consider themselves to be sensitive or empathic.

Another significant trope that we see in popular culture is the contents of the tarot deck, or more to the point, the lack of contents. When you see tarot on TV or in the movies, you often only see the Major Arcana being used. If you are speaking with someone about tarot or are about to perform a reading for them for the first time, they may be surprised to find that there are more cards beyond the 'picture cards' that everyone recognizes. Explain that all the cards have a role to play and that they all depend on the others to help tell a full, accurate story.

When people understand the role of the deck, they will have a better understanding of the tarot as a whole. You certainly don't have to go into a recitation of every card in your deck during every conversation, but telling people you know that the Death card makes for good television while explaining that there are dozens of other cards should be sufficient to open the dialogue. People who want to know more will ask for elaboration, which of course, you'll be happy to give!

Debunk the Negativity

There is also a negative connotation attached to tarot in terms of the use of the word occult. You are going to meet people who have a visceral negative reaction because they think that tarot, and the occult, are in direct opposition to religion. Some will go so far as to say they think that the tarot is connected to Satanism. As a general rule, it isn't. Tarot belongs to no religions and at the same time, all religions, and that's the answer you can give.

How is this possible? Simply put, tarot belongs to the people who utilize it. If those people include both tarot and Satanism in their personal spirituality, then it is connected to Satanism through those people. If a tarot practitioner is a Jew, a Buddhist, an atheist, a pagan, or a Catholic, then the tarot belongs to that faith. Remember, the images on some of the earliest tarot decks were pulled straight from Christian artwork. There was a time when tarot *was* directly tied to a religion. As tarot spread across the world and evolved, it became attached and detached from religious sects on a regular basis. Therefore, tarot belongs to both all and no religions. The art of tarot rests solely on the preferred spirituality of the individual reader.

There are religious leaders in all religions who use tarot cards for guidance. Some have specific decks commissioned to reflect the imagery of their religion and use these to meditate and pray for insight and intention. To say that tarot is attached to any specific religion is to discount that tarot is for everyone. Tarot can bridge the divide between this world and the next while keeping us grounded in the reality of our earthly existence, and that's also what religion strives to do. To say that tarot and religion are at odds with another or cannot coexist without a fully-defined connection is ignorant. Religion and tarot are never mutually exclusive, nor do they need to be intrinsically linked.

One last stereotype we'll discuss is that of the modern tarot reader. This may be the only stereotype you wish to play into rather than debunk, and that's the stereotype of the mystic. We'll talk about building a tarot business in a little while, and why being a mystic might be a persona you want to use for entertainment purposes. But if you want to, you can slough off the idea that tarot readers are, for lack of a better term, weird. Of course, we are- but so is everyone else on this planet.

Tarot *is* a bit of a strange hobby or vocation, and it does take a certain type of person to get involved with reading the cards. But that doesn't mean you aren't also just a regular person who goes about their business, takes care of their kids, and live a relatively normal life. You can choose to make tarot as big or as small a part of your life as you feel comfortable with, and you don't owe anyone an explanation about it. That being said, when people ask, you may feel compelled to share your tarot journey. Talk to them about how and why you read tarot, where it fits into your greater spiritual lifestyle, and how it's been a blessing to you. The more people understand, the less they fear. This goes for tarot cards and for everything else in your life.

Building a Following

If you want to read tarot for other people, how do you get started? Whether for fun or for profit, you need to let people know that you are a tarot reader, and you're going to want to tap into the power of the internet. There are so many platforms that you can use, so how can you know what works and what doesn't? Let's take a look at some possibilities so you can decide what you're comfortable with and what will work for you.

Websites and Mailing Lists

Websites are a good way to establish a permanent web presence, and they can be inexpensive to purchase, build, and maintain if you know how or if you're capable of hiring someone with that knowledge. Of course, having a site isn't quite enough these days. You need it to be appealing, user-friendly, and accessible. The other thing is, people need to know that it's there! A blog is a good place to start if you're unsure about what type of website you need. Blogs are easy to edit and can be laid out cleanly with little internet experience. There are some excellent, affordable blog platforms that anyone can learn how to use. Choose an uncomplicated username, purchase your domain, and get started!

Once you've secured your site, a great next step is to build a mailing list. This will help you sign people up and draw them into your tarot services. You can create a mailing list organically by asking your family and friends to sign up and then forward your emails to their other friends and so on until you've gained a following. You can also, relatively inexpensively, buy mailing lists from brokers. You want to find a reputable third-party broker, one that lets you specify the interests of the people you are seeking to add. The more targeted you can be with your email marketing, the more likely you are to build a dedicated following.

Marketing doesn't have to be difficult, and email marketing is made simpler every day by subscription programs that allow you to plug in your content and hit send. The work that you put in dictates the results that you will get back. Be bright and brief, offer people something unique, and fill a need and a niche. By the time you're ready to market your tarot skills to others, you are going to have your style and signature in place. Use this to your advantage and promote yourself and your tarot skills as a total package.

Social Media Success

Everyone is on social media these days. Facebook, Twitter, Instagram, TikTok, the list goes on and on. How can you put your tarot skills on display and make sure they are seen? The first thing you need to do is come up with a username that you can use across as many of these platforms as possible. This continuity allows people to find you on whichever site they choose to use and search for you easily on others. It may feel sad to say, but in today's fast-paced digital society, people don't want to put in the effort to click too many times. Being accessible and easy-to-find is a hallmark of social media success.

One of the biggest drivers of social media is videos and live content. People want to see action, not words. Create accounts that allow you to use video content to your advantage, and of course, link the accounts onto your webpage and into your mailing list emails. The more eyes you can get on your social media, the better. One word of warning about 'buying' followers. It sounds great in theory, but it's not always best in practice. Many of these so-called followers are bots, not real people. You can't read a computer program's tarot cards, so buying followers might not be the best return on your investment.

Instead, consider paying for social media advertisements or boosted/sponsored posts. You can fit this type of purchase into any budget, and you can target the specific demographic you want to attract. Every social media platform has an algorithm that determines how frequently a post shows up in a news feed. You want to bring in enough initial followers to get you over the hump of that algorithm so that your posts begin to get more organic exposure. If you can spend a little money to do that, you'll eventually be able to stop paying for people to see your content and start seeing a return on your investment.

You can also be bold and tag people whom you want to see your work. This is a good way to catch the eye of celebrities you admire that you think might be interested in what you have to offer. Tag business that deals in the mystical and the occult and see if they will share your work. Social media is all about who can grab the most attention, that's how things go viral and become popular. Don't be a shrinking violet when it comes to your posts. Add hashtags, stay upbeat, and grab positive attention any way you can.

Can Tarot Be a Viable Business?

That leads us to our next question- can reading the tarot be a viable business? The answer is absolutely, unequivocally, yes! Like any small business, you need to know your niche and what need you want to fill. If you've already set up a personal website and social media, then chances are good that you've figured that out. Your tarot persona is what you are going to be selling to people, so who are the people you want to sell to? Are you a middle-class mom who wants to get other moms into tarot? Are you the retired librarian who wants to spread wisdom and guidance? Are you the classic mystic tarot reader who plays to the stereotype with a modern twist? Know who you are and who your customers are before you begin. Always check your local or state ordinances for any guidance on registering a business name, what type, if any, of incorporation you need, and what type of service category reading tarot falls under. You may be subject to permitting or licensing if you're going to entertain customers in your home. You should also look into basic business liability insurance, regardless of your chosen service model.

Making Money Online

Making money online is easier than ever these days, but you have to be savvy and decisive about how you build a website for this purpose. How will you offer tarot readings over the internet? Will you also sell tarot cards and guides? How about any other value-added products or accessories, like crystals or smudge sticks? These are all things to consider before you begin. You should carefully investigate some e-commerce providers to choose the best host for your website. You may even be able to migrate your personal page or blog content over to your new business site.

To have a tarot business online, you'll need a platform for performing readings and one for accepting payments. There are so many available video conferencing platforms these days, you can choose the one that's best for your needs, and membership plans are fairly inexpensive for some of the more popular, reliable platforms. Your website will also need to include many of the things you might also offer in-person; this could include a guide to the interpretation of cards, a history of tarot, and a shopping page for books, cards, and accessories. For payment, choose the option that works best for your bank account. Depending on what bank you have, PayPal, CashApp, Venmo, or Zelle, are all viable options.

You might also consider accepting credit cards, although there are usually fees involved with the processing.

When you transfer a personal art like tarot to a fully-online platform, be aware that you may lose some of the elements that come with a live tarot reading. There is also an added level of trust from your clients, especially if you are offering personalized reading via email or phone, as well as through live video-conferencing. These subjects are trusting that you will perform a true, accurate reading for them based on the information they provided. Don't violate that trust! Perform every reading, live or not, as if the client were sitting right in front of you. You'll stay in practice, and you'll not be tempted to put forth less effort.

Brick-and-Mortar in the Modern Era

Times are tough for small businesses, but that doesn't mean you can't start a successful brick-and-mortar tarot location. The best approach to doing this is to dream big and start small. You are one person and a deck of cards. Where can you work? Do you need a large solo storefront, or can you rent space inside another established business? Can you work from home? These are the first things to think about when you want to establish yourself in a fixed location.

If you want to work from home, you'll need a dedicated space if you want to be taken seriously. Is there a room in your house that can be a 'tarot office'? What about an outbuilding like a big shed? You can decide this on your own, but think about whether or not you would like your cards to be read in a space that is clearly set up for the purpose, or at someone's kitchen table while their kids run around screaming. The answer isn't too hard to arrive at. When working from home, you need space to actually be able to work.

If you're looking to get out of the house and into a commercial space, it might be in your best interest to rent space in an existing business like an occult shop or spiritual items supplier. Look at listings in your area for these types of businesses. If all you need is some space to decorate a corner, and you're willing to pay the business owner to be there a few days a week, they might jump on the money. You are adding value to their business and helping offset the rent or mortgage, all while building your clientele. It's a win-win.

Acquiring your own commercial property is the most expensive of the brick-and-mortar prospects. It's also the biggest commitment. Before you buy or lease a commercial storefront, consider all the factors. What will happen if things don't work out? Are you financially able to make payments on a property that you might not be utilizing? Is this location suitable for your type of business? You likely don't want to open a tarot shop in a warehouse district. That old cliché about location, location, location exists for a reason. You should look for something in a retail shopping district. Perhaps you live in or near a small town that has a Main Street economic district. These properties often have incentives or tax breaks to keep the storefronts full.

Another thing to consider is the scope of your business. How much room do you possibly need to perform your readings? Will you also be offering retail products like cards, accessories, or even branded apparel? This needs to be factored into both your space and your monetary budget. Remember, it will cost you less money to begin with very little and work your way into bigger things than to start with high overhead and product costs and try to make that money back.

No matter how you choose to build a brick-and-mortar business, save yourself stress by making sure you get all the necessary permits, insurance, and business registration forms you need before you set up shop. You'll save time, money, and headaches in the short- and long-term.

Fairs and Festivals for Classic Flair

If you don't want to work from your home or in a commercial location, the third option is to become a traveling tarot reader. You can market your skills at craft fairs, street festivals, renaissance faires, trade shows, and outdoor concerts. For most of these types of events, all you'll need to do is rent a vendor space and set up shop. Some states may require a peddler's permit, but you can ask the event coordinator if this is necessary when you inquire about registering.

This option is appealing for many reasons. If you like to travel, you can go as far away from home as you are comfortable with, and that will be cost-effective. You can participate in these events with little overhead costs, other than travel expenses and your supplies, as you may need to bring your own table, chairs, and tent, and you are going to want to have some modicum of décor, like a wall hanging, banner, and tablecloth. Registration for fairs and festivals vary widely by the size and popularity of the event but don't discount an event based on those factors.

If you have to pay a premium for your space, that's likely a good indicator that the event draws a big crowd. You should be able to make your money back quite easily, and you can research what type of demographic usually attends the event and adjust your prices accordingly. If you're attending a small event, make yourself a big deal there! Offer specials and draw in as many customers as you can. Ask people to sign up for your mailing list and talk about their experience with you on social media. Be part of the reason a small event grows and becomes successful.

You can have amazing experiences traveling and practicing your art, and you'll make amazing friends and connections along the way. Even if you don't make a full-time job from your tarot reading, you can make some nice pocket money by attending one of two events a month. If you're not sure how to get started with working events, start small. Check out the calendars in the local media outlets in your area. They will be chock full of press releases for groups looking for vendors for various craft fairs, street festivals, tricky trays, and holiday shops. Get in touch and take the leap; you might just get hooked on the experience.

No matter how you choose to build a tarot-based business, the most important thing to remember is that you are building a following at all times. You want to drive repeat business by making an impression with your storytelling style, your fashion sense, and of course, your accuracy and demeanor while reading the cards. You want to be the tarot reader that people seek out at an annual street fair or the one that someone emails from the other side of the globe for an online reading. Be the tarot reader that people travel to your town to see. If you can practice your craft with belief and integrity while also embracing the ideals of modern marketing, you will find wild success in your tarot business endeavors.

Preserving and Promoting Tarot for the Future

Tarot can only continue to survive and thrive in the coming centuries through the efforts of people like you who care deeply about the art. It's not enough to just be a teacher; you also need to be a promoter and proponent and supporter of other tarot practitioners, and a vocal advocate for the preservation of the artwork and history.

Be a Teacher

One of the best ways to ensure that the art of tarot lives on is to pass your skills and knowledge on to others. If you have an established tarot reading business, you can offer lessons and guidance to others who wish to learn how to practice tarot on their own. You can offer full courses or individual lessons, or offer an online subscription service. There are a lot of ways to teach tarot and still support your business.

If you can, get involved with youth organizations or community-based groups to offer a tarot night. Develop educational materials that can be used for students of all ages and deliver them at local libraries and community clubs. Offer to be part of the cocktail hours of fundraising galas. There are so many ways to bring tarot to people of any age or demographic, and you can focus on what that demographic might like to learn about. Give presentations about the artwork to art students. Talk about the history of tarot at the local museum. Whatever opportunities you have to expose new people to the art of tarot, you should take them. It is through these actions that more people will take an interest in the practice and decide to take it up.

Be a Student and Supporter

Whatever your tarot-style, you will always meet people who can teach you something new. We've based this book on the Rider Waite System, but there are any number of other systems, decks, and styles out there just waiting to be learned. The more you practice tarot, the more inclined you will be to branch out into new decks and systems. Eventually, you will want to build your own decks, so find people you can turn to for guidance on systems and artwork. You can also continue to watch and visit with other tarot readers to learn from their experience and expertise.

The artwork itself is another great way that you can be a supporter of tarot. Seek out new artists creating deck designs. To be a tarot deck illustrator means a great deal of dedication to the craft. These artists are working with all sorts of media, from pen and ink, paint and brush, and digital art programs, and the art they are producing is stunning. If you attend tarot conferences or gatherings, pay attention to the artists promoting their decks, and if you can't purchase their work, at least snag their information, and support the ones you like on social media.

You can join organizations if you like, but be sure to vet them before spending your membership money. Do they work within the tarot community to promote the art? Where do your membership dues go? What benefits do they offer to their members? Do they work harmoniously in the tarot world, or do they bash other groups? You don't have to join a group to be a respected tarot reader, so if you don't feel comfortable joining a group or guild, don't! Just make sure that if you do, they are reputable and are working towards the betterment and benefit of their members and the art of tarot.

Don't discount the power of the online community. You can find plenty of like-minded tarot readers from all over the world to share ideas and experiences with, no official membership required. If you've built a tarot business, you could even create your own forum on your website where people can learn and talk freely amongst themselves. This also gives you an opportunity to share your knowledge in a less formal setting.

Be a Historian

The history at the beginning of this book is just a glimpse into the rich past of the tarot deck. Studying the history of tarot is a hobby of itself, and you can lose yourself in the styles, the artwork, and the interpretation guides as they developed over the centuries. If you're able, traveling to the birthplaces of tarot and seeing people playing card games with replica decks is an experience all tarot readers should have at least once. While you're there, you can ask to be taught the games and familiarize yourself with another use of the cards.

You can focus your study of tarot history on a specific century or country, learning all you can about a regional variation or evolution of the cards. The art history alone is a fascinating subject, so if you have a love of art or artistic tendencies, you can become an expert in all things related to tarot art. There are deck designs that deserve preservation and are nearly lost to the ravages of time. You can even try your hand at recreating the art that you find the most appealing and building your own deck. When you are familiar with the past, you can continue to do justice to the art of tarot for the future.

Be an Advocate

Get on a soapbox! Be vocal about your love of tarot and what it means to you. Talk to people about it at dinner parties, at the gym, at yoga class, at the bus stop waiting for the kids...you get the idea. Being an advocate of tarot means that you are willing to discuss the practice with anyone willing to listen. Use personal experience and talk about how tarot has changed your life for the better. You can talk about tarot in a way that appeals to the person you're talking to; remember, you should be able to read people like you read the cards.

Some people will be receptive to your conversations, and some might fall into that category of skeptics whose minds just can't be changed. That's okay, too. You shouldn't force anyone into an uncomfortable conversation. When you talk about tarot, frame it in a positive light, and talk about the benefits of having your cards read. Explain what tarot means as a part of your spiritualism, and if people bring up religion, you can break up that stereotype. As for those, do everything you can to debunk them. People tend to be apprehensive of things they don't understand, and it's often the word 'occult' that makes them nervous. By being a proud tarot reader and a vocal advocate for the art, you can bust a lot of stereotypes and break down barriers for the betterment of the art.

Be a Role Model

If you want to preserve and promote tarot for the future, be someone that others can look up to today. This means being a fair and accurate reader, an ardent student and teacher, and someone who works with the art with integrity and respect. You should put your all into every reading you perform, and give people the readings they need and deserve. Learn everything you can about harnessing your emotional energy to be the best reader you can be.

Rely on your fundamentals and revisit them often. When you are invested in your craft, it will show in your work and earn you respect. Build a reputation as someone who is not only intuitive and skilled but open to sharing the art of tarot with those who would learn. The best thing you can do to promote tarot is to be someone who immerses themselves into the cards and not only understands how to interpret them, but how to relate them to modern life. The cards and their meanings may be centuries old, but you need to move with the times.

Be someone who sticks to their word when it comes to promoting the art of tarot. If you build an online following and promise your subscribers a gift or a single card reading every day, follow through on your intentions. The only way to keep tarot alive, show skeptics that the cards are a real tool for divination, and pass along your knowledge to the next generation of readers and artists is to be honest, perform your art with integrity, and work toward being a pillar of the tarot community.

We're coming to the end of our time together, and we just want to leave you with a brief recap of how you can become a proficient, accurate, respected tarot reader. Learn your history and study your cards, their artwork, and their meanings. The more you study, the quicker your recall will become when you are interpreting the cards. Practice your layouts and deals, and take good care of your cards. Learn to be compassionate and open with the people who've come to you for help, and protect yourself from overwhelming emotions.

If you choose to build a tarot business, do so with the best of intentions and with integrity and respect for the art. Promote and preserve the tarot for the next generations by being the best tarot reader you can be, and pass your knowledge on to others who would learn. Be ardent in your practice, your readings, and your support of the craft, and may you be blessed with intuition and accuracy for all your readings to come.

CONCLUSION

Thank you so much for reading *Tarot for Dummies*! We hope you enjoyed the book and learned everything you need to know about getting started with the art of reading tarot. It's been a lot of fun to provide you with this information.

Whether you want to read tarot for fun or for profit, or even if you just appreciate the history and the artwork of the tarot deck, you now have the fundamentals to go out, get your very first deck (how exciting!), and get some hands-on practice of studying the tarot cards. They are an entity of themselves. You will feel a connection to them as if they were a friend, and indeed, some tarot readers claim a strong bond with their cards that cannot be described as less than true friendship.

The preservation of the history of tarot and the future of the art depends a lot on people like you, who have chosen to educate themselves about this most venerated of card games that became a tool of divination at the hands of Victorian-era scholars and showmen. This enduring legacy deserves to live on, and the mystery and aura of the cards should be left in the hands of the people who most respect and appreciate it, and that's the tarot readers themselves. By studying, reading, and teaching the art of tarot, you can be a small piece of those centuries of history.

The best advice that we can leave you with is to be proud of your love of tarot. You can continue to bust stereotypes, teach the history and the transformation of the tarot deck, immerse yourself in the thousands of different artistic styles available today, or be a purist about what the aesthetic of the cards should be. Don't hide or be ashamed of your tarot skills; it is an art worthy of preserving from a historical, occult, and artistic standpoint.

We hope that you can take all that you've read here and become a proficient, intuitive tarot card reader and that the art of tarot enriches your life in many ways. Reading the tarot cards makes you a better storyteller, both in content and style. It makes you feel more connected to the world around you and the people who ask for your reading expertise. Reading the tarot also connects you indelibly to the past and the future, and that may be the most important thing.

We all want to find our place in the universe. Tarot can help you with that, both as the subject and as the reader. It's a powerful spiritual and decision-making tool, and when you have tarot reading skills, you open yourself up to that world of possibilities. With that, we thank you once again for reading *Tarot for Dummies*. Please come back and study the pages again and again for meanings, to try different layouts, and to refresh yourself about using your intuition and finding your voice. Enjoy your tarot journey! We're so glad you started it with us.

DESCRIPTION

The historical art of tarot passed down for centuries through nobility and showmen can now be at your fingertips with this easy-to-read guide to *Tarot for Dummies*. If you have ever wanted to learn how to deal, interpret, and study reading tarot cards, then this is the book, based on the ever-popular Rider Waite System, for you. In this four-part volume, you will find:

- the history of tarot from its origins as a deck of game-play cards in the 14th century

- a look at the evolution of tarot from a game to a tool for divination

- an explanation of the contents of a modern tarot deck

- lists including the upright and reversed meanings of all 78 cards

- information about the tarot suits and their standard playing deck counterparts

- the differences and the purposes of the Major and Minor Arcana

- a detailed description of the artwork on each standard tarot card

- a wide variety of deals and layouts, with sample queries and interpretations

- instructions and guidance on how to shuffle, deal, and interpret the cards

- advice on talking to your subjects before reading their cards

- lessons on intuition, demeanor, style, and aesthetics

- encouragement on using intuition and 'gut feelings'

- a look at modern applications of tarot

- a glimpse at how tarot is portrayed in popular culture

- and so much more!

Tarot for Dummies isn't just a list of cards and meanings; it is a comprehensive guide to learning about what it means to be a tarot card reader in the age of technology. This book will show you how to handle skepticism, criticism, and stereotypes. It will teach you how to be both a reader of cards and a reader of people, how to prepare and practice to gain proficiency, and how to avoid being overcome with the emotions of those whose cards you are reading. This is especially important information not only for empaths and other highly-sensitive tarot readers but for everyone who wants to read tarot or have a reading done for them.

Tarot for Dummies also addresses other modern concerns, like building a tarot business or social media following online, how to approach having a brick-and-mortar business, or how to find a following on the fair and festival scene to earn income from tarot as a side business. It also talks about the obligations of a tarot reader to be accurate, honest, and informative in every reading to preserve the integrity of the art and gives tips on how to get your subjects to be specific in their queries and appeals.

If you are looking for an easy-to-read, all-inclusive primer on the art of tarot, then you need to look no further than *Tarot for Dummies*. It's sure to become your favorite reference for learning the meanings of the tarot cards and the true meaning of being a tarot card reader. Get your copy today, and get started with a fulfilling, engrossing, life-changing hobby. You'll be so glad you did!

www.ingramcontent.com/pod-product-compliance
Lightning Source LLC
Chambersburg PA
CBHW071431070526
44578CB00001B/73